The Expert Witness Handbook

THE EXPERT WITNESS HANDBOOK—A Guide for Engineers
Second Edition

Printed in the United States of America

ISBN: 0-912045-03-5

Professional Publications, Inc.
1250 Fifth Avenue, Belmont, CA 94002
(650) 593-9119
www.ppi2pass.com

Current printing of this edition: 5

The EXPERT WITNESS Handbook

—A Guide for Engineers—

Second Edition

PROFESSIONAL PUBLICATIONS, INC.
Belmont, CA 94002

In the ENGINEERING REFERENCE MANUAL SERIES

Engineer-In-Training Reference Manual
Engineering Fundamentals Quick Reference Cards
Engineer-In-Training Sample Examinations
Mini-Exams for the E-I-T Exam
1001 Solved Engineering Fundamentals Problems
E-I-T Review: A Study Guide
Diagnostic F.E. Exam for the Macintosh
Fundamentals of Engineering Video Series:
  Thermodynamics
Civil Engineering Reference Manual
Civil Engineering Quick Reference Cards
Civil Engineering Sample Examination
Civil Engineering Review Course on Cassettes
101 Solved Civil Engineering Problems
Seismic Design of Building Structures
Seismic Design Fast
Timber Design for the Civil P.E. Exam
Fundamentals of Reinforced Masonry Design
246 Solved Structural Engineering Problems
Mechanical Engineering Reference Manual
Mechanical Engineering Quick Reference Cards

Mechanical Engineering Sample Examination
101 Solved Mechanical Engineering Problems
Mechanical Engineering Review Course on
  Cassettes
Consolidated Gas Dynamics Tables
Fire and Explosion Protection Systems
Electrical Engineering Reference Manual
Electrical Engineering Quick Reference Cards
Electrical Engineering Sample Examination
Chemical Engineering Reference Manual
Chemical Engineering Quick Reference Cards
Chemical Engineering Practice Exam Set
Land Surveyor Reference Manual
1001 Solved Surveying Fundamentals Problems
Land Surveyor-In-Training Sample Examination
Engineering Economic Analysis
Engineering Law, Design Liability, and
  Professional Ethics
Engineering Unit Conversions

In the ENGINEERING CAREER ADVANCEMENT SERIES

How to Become a Professional Engineer
The Expert Witness Handbook— A Guide for Engineers
Getting Started as a Consulting Engineer
Intellectual Property Protection— A Guide for Engineers
E-I-T/P.E. Course Coordinator's Handbook
Becoming a Professional Engineer
Engineering Your Start-Up
High-Technology Degree Alternatives
Metric in Minutes

THE EXPERT WITNESS HANDBOOK—A Guide for Engineers
Second Edition

Printed in the United States of America

ISBN: 0-912045-03-5

Professional Publications, Inc.
1250 Fifth Avenue, Belmont, CA 94002
(415) 593-9119

Current printing of this edition: 4

Revised and reprinted in 1995.

TABLE OF CONTENTS

Preface v

Acknowledgments vii

What is an Expert Witness? 1

Who Can Be an Expert Witness? 2

What Are the Functions of the Expert Witness? 3

Who Are the Forensic Engineer's Clients? 4

What Does the Expert Witness Actually Do? 6

The Preliminary Investigation 7

The Technical Investigation 9

Report of the Investigation 13

The Discovery Process 13

Discovery and the Expert Witness 16
    The Interrogatory 16
    The Subpoena 16
    The Deposition 18
    The Pre-Deposition Conference 19
    Giving a Deposition 20
    Uses of the Deposition 22
    What are Depositions For? 23
    Your Rights as a Witness 24
    Rights Generally Applicable 24

Credibility as a Deponent 30

Testifying in Court 34
    Preparing to Testify 34
    Before Testimony 36
    Stages of the Examination 37
    Establishing Qualification as an Expert 37
    Rules of Evidence 38

The Direct Examination 39
The Cross-Examination 41
The Redirect and Recross Examinations 47
After Testimony 48

Closing Out the Case 49

A Note on Arbitration 49

Administration and Management of the Forensic Case 51
Screening the Case 51
Fees 51
The Contract 53
Fees Charged to Opposing Counsel 54

Forensic Engineering as a Business 54
Establishing a Reputation as an Expert 55
Finding Referrals 57
How Much of Your Practice Should Be Devoted to
    Forensic Engineering? 59
Management Issues in Forensic Engineering 61

Ethical Considerations 63

Could You Be a Forensic Engineer? 64

Suggested Reading 65

Bibliography 67

Appendix A
    Sample Contract: Individual Consultant or Small Firm 69

Appendix B
    Sample Contract: Large Engineering Firm 71

Appendix C
    Addresses of Professional Agencies and Associations 75

Appendix D
    Conducting a Literature Search 77

Index

PROFESSIONAL PUBLICATIONS, INC.   Belmont, CA

PREFACE

This book is an introduction to the world of the expert witness, or forensic engineer. It will be of interest to any engineer who is curious about the work of expert witnesses, and it will be especially valuable for those of you who are considering a venture into the field of forensic engineering.

The book describes the role and functions of the expert witness and outlines the qualifications necessary for success in this field. It will take you step by step through the activities of a forensic engineer, offering practical recommendations at every step.

The book discusses the legal procedures you are likely to encounter as an expert witness, defining terms and indicating what you can expect at every stage of a litigation. It gives suggestions on how to prepare for testimony and how to behave on the witness stand. It shows you what to look out for in selecting a case, what precautions to take in conducting an investigation, and how to manage a forensic engineering practice.

After reading this book, you will be able to evaluate your own potential for success in the field of forensic engineering. Even if you do not elect to specialize in this field, the increasing trend toward product-failure litigation makes it very possible that you will be invited to serve as an expert witness sometime in your career. In such an event, this book will aid you in performing the job professionally and successfully.

In scanning engineering journals and magazines, you have probably encountered articles with intriguing titles like "Forensic Engineering," "The Engineer in the Courtroom," or "Engineers as Expert Witnesses." If you are fascinated by the law and the drama of the courtroom, or more practically, if you are attracted by what one author has called the "prestige way to moonlight," you may wonder what this business of forensic engineering or expert witnessing is all about.

This book will answer some of your questions, such as: Who can be an expert witness? What does the expert witness actually do? How does the expert witness prepare to testify? What can the expert witness expect in the courtroom? How can testimony be made more effective? What are the ethical responsibilities of the expert witness? How can the expert witness find clients? What are the appropriate financial arrangements? You will find answers to these questions, and many others, in the pages to follow.

WHAT IS AN EXPERT WITNESS? It has been noted that the United States is an increasingly litigious society—more and more people are going to court over more and more issues. A large share of these legal proceedings originate with individuals or corporate entities who have suffered physical, financial, or other damage when some structure or industrial product failed. Who is responsible in these cases—the designer? the manufacturer or builder? the user or consumer? Often the courts must decide.

The courts, however, are handicapped in making these judgments by the fact that many modern structures and products are exceedingly complex. The adversary procedures of the courtroom are founded on essentially equalitarian assumptions. The principle of a jury of peers, for instance, assumes basically similar stores of knowledge, common sense, and capacity for judgment among citizens. Increasingly, understanding how structures or products are or should be designed, built, and used requires a great deal of technical knowledge which is not available to the average person. A typical product-liability case involves large amounts of technical information which the judge, the jury, and even the contesting attorneys may fail to comprehend adequately. Courtroom procedures which were designed to produce just solutions to disputes under more normal conditions may founder in a morass of poorly-understood terminology and information.

Under these circumstances, it is not surprising that one or both parties to a dispute, or the court itself, may call upon experts who have the information, skills, and experience necessary to render an opinion as to the cause of product failure. Frequently the expert is an engineer whose training and experience qualify him or her to determine the cause of a failure. The expert's observations and opinions are presented in court as evidence in the case.

WHO CAN BE AN EXPERT WITNESS? An expert witness may be called when a question is not "resolvable by common knowledge," but instead requires "special knowledge, skill, experience, training or education" (California Evidence Code, Section 720). Depending on the nature of the case, various kinds of experts may be called upon to testify: ballistics experts, as we all know from newspapers and the movies, but also architects, psychologists, medical doctors, or almost any other type of specialist. In product failure cases, the relevant expert is most frequently an engineer.

Although the law does not require a professional license of the expert witness, in practice it is usually licensed professional engineers who are invited to testify as experts. There are at least three reasons for this. First, a licensed professional may carry more weight and credibility than an engineer who does not have a license. Second, only with a license can an engineer make himself available to the public for consulting services. Therefore, the chances of an unlicensed engineer being sought as an expert witness are very small. Third, an engineer who is not in a position to budget his or her own time may not be able to devote sufficient time to investigation and other aspects of a case. The first step in becoming a forensic (courtroom) engineer, then, is to become a licensed consulting engineer.

Beyond the license, which is made mandatory by the demands of practicality, and the special qualifications which are demanded by the law, the expert witness in any legal case will be individually examined for competency in that case. In order for the testimony of the expert witness to be acceptable as evidence, the court must rule that the witness's education and experience qualify him or her as an expert in that particular case. That is, expertise in engineering is not enough; the expertise must be directly relevant to the question at hand.

WHAT ARE THE FUNCTIONS OF THE EXPERT WITNESS?
In litigation involving product liability or similar questions, the court seeks to answer certain questions. Does or did the defendant owe any duty to the plaintiff, contractual or otherwise? Was there a breach of duty? Was the damage claimed by the plaintiff caused by the breach of duty? How much was the damage? The most important function of the expert witness is to offer opinions on technical matters bearing on these questions, which would otherwise be difficult or impossible for the judge or jury to assess properly.

In order to fulfill this function, you must fully understand the role of the expert witness. You must also become aware of relevant laws and other legal regulations, including those governing contracts and work agreements, and how they apply to engineering works.

There are other, less obvious functions of the expert witness. One of these functions was a prime consideration for the authors of the laws and regulations governing the employment of expert witnesses: their use helps to reduce the number of cases that actually go to trial. Pretrial investigations frequently make it clear which way the case is likely to go. A defendant who sees that he is probably going to lose in court will usually try to settle out of court, and a plaintiff who sees little chance of winning can save time, trouble, and expense by dropping the case or accepting a lower level of compensation.

Since both sides have access to a good deal of what the expert witness plans to say before the trial begins, both have the opportunity to evaluate the situation and decide whether or not to press the case. Only a small proportion of liability cases are pursued all the way to the courtroom, and the use of technical experts is an important factor in keeping that proportion low.

Another function of the expert witness is to lend credibility to the argument being advanced by one side or the other, over and above the pure information value of the testimony. In many cases, the greatest expert on a particular question may be the engineer who designed or built the product. However, the counsel for the opposition is almost certain to attack the designer's credibility on grounds of special interest. Who can be expected to impugn his own product, or to testify against an employer or customer? Likewise, an engineer associated with the plaintiff, as employee or in any other role, may not be persuasive as a witness, since his or her testimony may be attributed to company loyalty or other interests. Therefore, both sides may find it preferable to engage the more objective and credible outside expert as witness.

Although the main burden of the expert's testimony is concerned with the specific incident of failure which led to the suit or trial, part of it may be directed toward placing the failure in perspective. Was the structure or product designed, built, or manufactured in accordance with accepted practices, and did its performance meet accepted standards? Assignment of blame and responsibility may often rest as much on assessments of this sort as on technical analyses of what happened. Once again, the expert witness may be the most appropriate and credible source of opinions on such matters.

WHO ARE THE FORENSIC ENGINEER'S CLIENTS?   In most cases in which an expert witness is called, the person who first contacts the witness is an attorney representing one of the parties to a lawsuit. The largest single group of clients, then, consists of attorneys. However, an attorney may represent many different types of clients, and may approach the prospective witness in a variety of ways, from pretrial consultation to midtrial subpoena.

The attorney for a plaintiff may contact a consulting engineer for assistance in determining whether a case for professional negligence, unsafe design, or defective manufacture can be made. The attorney for the defendant may seek assistance from an engineer in exactly the same assessments, but may also be seeking evidence that the plaintiff and/or external conditions (e.g., temperature, visibility, etc.) might be held responsible for the product failure. Regardless of the different aims of the different sides in a suit, however, the professional engaged by either plaintiff or defendant must investigate and report the evidence objectively.

Who are the actual parties to these disputes? The claims brought are quite various, ranging from malpractice or professional negligence suits, to all types of construction claims, to product failure and liability claims. The plaintiff may be any entity which believes itself to have sustained loss or damage, from an individual or group of individuals to a large corporation. The defendant may be any entity whose suspected negligence or other fault may have led to the loss or damage sustained by the plaintiff. Typical defendants in these cases include architects, engineers, contractors, owners of buildings or other structures, manufacturers, utility companies, oil and mining companies, transport companies, government agencies at local, state and federal levels, and insurance companies.

It is more common for the defendant than the plaintiff to engage an expert, for at least two reasons. First, the defendant is more likely to be a large business entity whose resources can more easily cover the expense of an expert witness. Second, the defendant may stand to lose a great deal by losing the suit, and so may be more willing to undertake the extra expense. As pointed out earlier, the timely advice of a technical expert can help the client decide whether or not to settle out of court, and the difference between court-awarded damages and an out-of-court settlement may be well worth the investment.

Insurance companies constitute a second group of clients. An insurance company, which will initiate contact through a claims representative or an attorney, may enter the picture in a variety of ways. The defendant may be insured against the type of loss at question in the suit. In this case, not the defendant directly, but the insurance company stands to lose if the claim is successful. An insurance company in this situation may undertake the expenses of the defense, including the cost of an expert witness.

On the other hand, an insurance company may seek reimbursement from one or more responsible parties after paying a claim, and it may retain a technical expert to assess the cause of failure and determine responsibility for it. An insurance company may foresee that a legal suit against a party that it has insured is inevitable. In this case, it may seek technical assistance even before litigation proceedings are begun.

Where a suit appears feasible to the prospective plaintiff, or likely to the prospective defendant and/or the defendant's insurance carrier, the party which anticipates litigation may retain an expert against the possibility that evidence may later decay, be destroyed, or otherwise become unavailable. Thus, if one of the parties to a potential dispute has the foresight to engage an expert while the evidence is still intact, the expert may carry out an investigation and prepare testimony months or—given the usual delays in the court system—years before a suit is filed or brought to court.

A third potential type of client is the court itself. If it appears that expert testimony will be necessary for the resolution of a case, the court may appoint an expert or experts at any point before or during a trial. The court may require that the parties to litigation bear the cost of the expert's investigation, report, and testimony, or it may compensate the expert directly. A court-appointed expert witness is a "friend of the court" and does not function as a witness for either plaintiff or defendant.

A fourth category of potential clients consists of individuals who wish to bring claims for damage and who wish expert opinion on the merits of their case. Although the consulting engineer must evaluate every client carefully before acceptance, the individual claimant requires especially close scrutiny. Ordinarily, such an individual should obtain legal counsel first, before attempting to investigate the technical aspects of the case. The attorney then may or may not engage an expert witness, according to the requirements of the case. The cost of retaining an expert witness, including the investigation procedures, is beyond the means of most individuals. The forensic engineer should come to a clear understanding on the subject of fees, and preferably require a retainer fee, when dealing with an individual client.

WHAT DOES THE EXPERT WITNESS ACTUALLY DO? The job of the expert witness is not restricted to giving testimony in court. In fact, the time spent in court may be only a small fraction of the time spent on a case. The engineer who has been approached for work as an expert witness will first carry out a preliminary investigation to determine whether or not the case is a suitable one, and to estimate the time and fees that may be involved. If the case is accepted, a full-scale investigation is required. Depending on the nature of the case, the investigation may be relatively simple or may require elaborate laboratory work. The results of the investigation will be presented in a preliminary report. Later, during pretrial discovery procedures, the expert witness may be subpoenaed, with or without documents and records relevant to the investigation, and may be examined by counsel for both parties to the litigation during deposition hearings. Before being called to the witness stand, there may be lengthy conferences with the client's attorney in preparation for testimony. Finally, the witness will be both directly examined and cross-examined under oath in the courtroom.

For the prospective expert witness who has never testified in court before, each of these steps may be unexpectedly complicated and time-consuming. Some of them, such as the discovery procedures and cross-examination in court, may hold unpleasant surprises for the unprepared witness. The next several sections will be devoted to explaining each step in the work of the expert witness, and some of the legal procedures involved. This information will help prepare you for what you are likely to encounter, and increase the chances that you will feel fulfilled rather than dismayed by your first courtroom experience.

THE PRELIMINARY INVESTIGATION

In the ideal case, a prospective client's attorney will contact you early in the preparations for trial. This will give you ample time for the investigations that you will have to carry out.

Your preliminary investigation should be oriented primarily to determining whether the client has a viable case and whether or not you want to take it. The first step is to learn precisely the nature of the case: What was the alleged loss or damage? What was the alleged cause? Why does the client want expert consultation? What types of evidence will be available to you in your investigations?

The answers to these questions should make it clear whether or not the case appears to be viable. The attorney, who is likely to be working on a contingency fee basis, will want to know as quickly as possible whether the case should be pursued or a quick settlement should be sought. Of course, you cannot be certain at this stage whether or not the evidence will support the client's case, but sometimes it is obvious that it will not. This is very valuable information for the attorney and client.

The answers to these questions should also make it clear whether or not your expertise is applicable to the case. If you are not fully qualified, do not take the case, no matter how attractive it may appear on other grounds. Otherwise, you risk the embarrassment of having your credibility impeached or having the court disqualify you and your testimony, leaving your client unable to present technical evidence in court. If you cannot take the case, try to refer the client to an expert who is qualified to help.

The preliminary investigation will probably allow you to decide whether an expert opinion will be useful in the case. If it will not, you should explain this to the client's attorney and decline to take the case.

Your preliminary investigation may make it apparent that you are qualified to form an opinion on only one aspect of the problem, and that another expert or experts will be needed to study the other aspects. You should inform the client's attorney that further expert opinion is required and indicate the type of expert that will be needed. If possible, refer the attorney to a competent expert in the appropriate field.

During your preliminary investigation, it is important to learn who is involved in the case. This means that you should learn not only the identity of your prospective client, but also that of the plaintiff and of all the attorneys retained by both sides. Any potential conflict of interest—for instance, previous business relations between your firm and that of the client, or one of the attorneys involved in the case—must be strictly avoided. Any relationship of this sort is certain to be brought out in court by the counsel for the opposition in an attempt to discredit your testimony. Where it appears that conflict of interest is a possible issue, refer the client to another suitable expert.

Occasionally, a prospective client or his attorney will be unwilling to submit full information, will give incongruous statements, or will otherwise arouse your suspicion. If there is any doubt about the ethical status of the case, it should be rejected.

Before committing yourself to a case, remember that you will have to work in close cooperation with the attorney at every stage, and you should feel at ease in the relationship. If you do not feel comfortable with the attorney, it is better to refuse the case. An attorney who appears careless, uncooperative, or otherwise objectionable constitutes a danger to your professional reputation, and should be avoided.

If, up to this point, the case appears to be an appropriate one for you, compare the scope of the investigation that the client wants with your estimate of what needs to be done to make a correct judgment. A clear agreement with the client's counsel as to what procedures may be employed and what they may cost is essential at this stage.

The final item in the preliminary investigation is the matter of fees. If you decide to accept the case, present the client and/or the attorney with an estimate of how much the full investigation will cost. State clearly your hourly or per diem fees for investigation, consultation, and testimony. Try to ascertain how much the client is willing to budget for expert testimony. If the budget would limit your investigations, try to determine whether the limited investigation would be sufficient to establish the case. If it would not, this should be explained clearly.

Most forensic engineers charge on an hourly or daily basis. Many require the payment of a retainer fee at the beginning of the work, against which the daily or hourly fee is counted until the retainer is used up. If, at that point, further work remains to be done, a new agreement on payment may be reached.

In setting fees, never make the amount contingent on the outcome of the case. It is your duty to form an impartial opinion, and your fee should be strictly determined by the amount of time and work you put into the case. It should have no relation to your findings or to the outcome of the case. Your credibility as an expert witness could be gravely undermined if it were shown that your fee was dependent on whether or not the client won the case.

It must be made clear to the client that your fees will be the same no matter what the outcome of the case. It must also be made clear that your fees will be the same no matter what the outcome of your investigation—whether or not your opinion will be favorable to the client's case. It is best to draw up a written agreement as to the basis of payment (by time or lump sum) which specifically states that the fee is not contingent on the outcome of the case.

THE TECHNICAL INVESTIGATION   Once agreement has been reached with the client regarding fees and the scope of the investigation, you are ready to put your skills as an engineering expert to work. Since the objects of investigation in product failure cases are so various, it is difficult to make any specific recommendations regarding methods of examination. However, some considerations generally apply.

First, because you are investigating an incident in the past which you could not directly observe and over which you had no control, you will probably not be able to construct a definitive proof regarding what happened. Rather, you will be constructing a hypothesis about the cause or causes of failure. In doing so, you must be alert to other possible hypotheses, and conduct your investigation in such a way as to eliminate inadequate hypotheses.

This means that you will need to examine evidence suggested by all the hypotheses you can imagine, not only the one you favor. It is probable that the counsel for the opposition will advance arguments for other hypotheses. Ideally, you should be prepared to meet them with disconfirming or contradictory evidence, and show that your opinion has the best basis in fact.

Second, an obvious point may possibly get lost in the search for the cause of failure. Before establishing a cause, it is first necessary to establish precisely what failed. It will also be necessary to convince the court that you have investigated the particular part or structure that failed, not merely some adjacent or similar part. Your testimony will be seriously compromised if this point cannot be made.

In order to meet these two requirements—that you have all the evidence, and that the evidence you have is relevant—you should start your investigation with all the sources of information that you can find. Ask for all the information that the attorney has. Get your client's report of the facts. Read the claim filed by the plaintiff. Read transcripts of depositions by witnesses to the incident. Try to obtain police, fire, insurance, or other reports. Study your client's documents and any documents that can be obtained from the other side. Study any physical evidence that exists.

Because the attorney will probably have access to information that would otherwise not be available to you, it is important for the two of you to work closely at this stage. The attorney's cooperation in providing you with all the relevant materials will be invaluable to your investigation.

In some cases, the physical evidence may no longer be available at the time you begin your investigation. For instance, it may have been destroyed by fire or explosion during the failure incident, or it may have been altered by weather or chemical processes, or the user or others may have inadvertently altered an object so that it is no longer useful as evidence. However, you will generally be able to examine the failed structure or product for evidence of the cause of failure.

In all probability, you will not inspect the evidence alone. The attorney who has engaged you will arrange for the inspection and should accompany you. Depending on the nature of the incident you are investigating, a number of other people may also be present. Counsel for the opposition may be there, with or without experts who may have been engaged by the opposition. Law enforcement officials may be present. You may find a videotape crew on the scene to record your inspection.

It is important to behave with decorum under these circumstances. You should avoid direct interaction with opposition counsel, experts, photographers, or video crew. Let all communication with them be handled by your client's attorney.

Perhaps the most important recommendation regarding the inspection of physical evidence is to maintain full and complete records of your procedures at every point. Take with you all the materials you anticipate you will need: paper and pencil, certainly, but also graph paper, a portable tape recorder for dictation, and a camera. Consulting engineers who handle many forensic cases usually keep a prepacked "doctor bag" of tools and equipment that they are likely to need when inspecting physical evidence.

Use your tools and recording equipment to record your observations on the spot. Do not depend on your memory, no matter how good you think it is; write, draw, photograph, or otherwise record what you see when you see it. Details that do not seem important at first glance may be useful later, so it is best to record comprehensively.

A photographic record is useful in many cases, particularly considering the perishability of the evidence over time. It is often helpful to take a series of photographs, beginning with the overall scene and working down to details of the failure. If there are labels, placards, instructions, or warnings posted on or near the evidence, be sure to photograph them and indicate their placement.

For each photograph, you should record all the relevant information: the object or part that was photographed, the date, the time of day, lighting conditions, the type of camera, the lens, the speed of the film, the distance and angle from which the shot was taken, and any other information that might affect the interpretation of the photograph. Each photograph in a series should be appropriately labeled with the direction and distance from which it was shot, as well as its order in the series.

Do not forget that months or even years may pass between the time the photographs are taken and the time you may be required to discuss them in court. A full record of all the circumstances surrounding the photographs will enable you to sound competent on the witness stand, rather than vague, confused, or forgetful. This precaution will also help to fore-stall any attempts to call into question the authenticity or relevance of the photographs.

The same principle of full recording applies to any other observation or measurement technique that you may use. When carrying out observations or measurements, try to anticipate all the questions that might be asked, and gather and record full information regarding each of them.

Simple inspection may not answer all the questions you have. You may need to perform tests to determine the cause of failure. If the tests will in any way change or damage the object being tested, it will be necessary to obtain consent from everyone involved in the litigation, from the opposition as well as from your client, and from any other technical experts who may have been engaged by either side. If alternative testing procedures are possible, you will also need to reach agreement with all sides as to what tests are to be performed using what procedures. It is usually not necessary to obtain consent to carry out nondestructive tests.

It is a good practice to establish a quality assurance program for all measuring tools that you routinely use in inspections or tests (e.g., calipers, micrometers, voltmeters, etc.). The program should describe your calibration procedures and measurement practices. Send your primary measuring tools to a calibration service on a regular basis. Measurements taken with instruments which are calibrated by stand-ards traceable to the National Bureau of Standards add credibility to your measurements and speak well for the quality of your work.

If you take evidence into your possession for any reason, protect it care-fully. You could be liable for the amount of the case if the evidence is lost or damaged without consent. When receiving or returning evidence, make sure that receipts specifying who has surrendered the evidence to whom are signed by both sides. While the evidence is in your possession, label or tag it with the case name, job number, or other identifying information. If there is more than one piece of evidence, keep an itemized list of all the evidence you have pertaining to the case.

In a few cases, the investigation may require the building of models or testing of analogous structures. Since model-building may be costly in terms of both time and materials, such a procedure should be fully discussed with the client and an agreement should be reached on the costs that will be entailed.

REPORT OF THE INVESTIGATION You will eventually write up the results of your investigation in a report. However, you should not commit anything to writing until asked to do so by the attorney. Instead, you should discuss your findings with the attorney. Any written report will be subject to discovery by other parties to the litigation.

If, on the basis of your investigation, you will not be able to give testimony favorable to your client's case, the attorney will probably decide not to designate you as an expert witness, and will not ask you for a written report. Your findings may or may not persuade the attorney to seek settlement out of court. On the other hand, if your findings appear to be useful, the attorney may ask you for a report of your findings and opinions, and, at some point in the preparations for trial, will designate you as an expert witness.

Regardless of the outcome of your investigation or the opinion that you form, and regardless of whether you will be retained as an expert witness, you should not reveal your findings or opinions to anyone other than the attorney who engaged you as consultant, except when giving testimony in a deposition or during trial.

After you have been designated as an expert witness, your written report will be subject to discovery. It is important, then, to prepare the report carefully, avoiding contradictions or ambiguities which could play into the hands of the opposition counsel. Not only your report, but also your notes and most of the contents of your file on the case may be subject to discovery procedures. In preparing drawings, notes, and other materials which will be part of your file, you should assume that they will be seen and read by the opposition attorneys, and you should exercise the requisite caution.

THE DISCOVERY PROCESS Discovery may be loosely defined as a set of procedures which allow any party or potential party to a lawsuit to obtain information bearing on the case. The details of discovery may vary somewhat according to whether the suit is being brought in federal or state court, and according to the state. The Federal Rules of Civil Procedure include rules governing discovery in actions brought in federal courts, and each state also has rules of civil procedure with regulations governing discovery in suits brought in that state. In general, the discovery process allows both sides to a litigation access to the same information and evidence before a trial.

The principle of allowing both sides access to each other's evidence may strike you as a bit strange if your courtroom experience has been mostly by way of movies and television. The surprise witness or the telling bit of evidence introduced at the last moment often constitutes the climax in courtroom dramas. However, real-life courts seek to minimize the dramatic and surprise elements in trials, and to maximize the speed and fairness with which civil disputes may be settled. They also seek to reduce the pressure of crowded court calendars and long backlogs of unsettled cases by discouraging litigation and encouraging settlement out of court. Legislatures have enacted discovery rules to help meet both of these concerns.

Discovery encourages settlement in several ways. Most fundamentally, it allows opposing attorneys to assess the strength of each other's claims by making information more fully available to both sides. Just as expert opinion can contribute to out-of-court settlement, discovery can also encourage the disputing parties to resolve their differences outside the courts.

Perhaps as important as the information pertaining to evidence which discovery makes available is the information pertaining to the parties and witnesses themselves. Each attorney has an opportunity to observe each witness while taking depositions, and to form an expectation as to how the witness will probably behave on the stand. Whether a witness appears knowledgeable, self-confident, and in command of the facts, or appears hesitant, unsure, and confused can be as influential on the jury as a piece of evidence or a legal argument.

Of course, not every dispute ends in settlement out of court. In cases that eventuate in legal action, discovery procedures can expedite both preparation for the trial and the trial itself.

Frequently, one side will have information or evidence that would be difficult or expensive for the other side to obtain. Discovery procedures reduce the time and expense involved in preparation for trial by making pretrial disclosure of evidence more likely.

If a case is a complex one, it may be difficult to foresee what the crucial issues will be. During discovery procedures, attorneys may be able to bring the issues into clearer focus and identify the significant facts and pieces of evidence. This will help to streamline questioning and arguments during the trial.

At the beginning of preparations for trial, the parties and witnesses may be somewhat vague in their reports and contentions. The process of repeated questioning in depositions and other discovery proceedings may help them to clarify their statements and solidify their commitment to their particular version of the facts. This in turn will help to minimize courtroom time that might be spent on wavering witnesses and the exploitation of uncertainties.

Discovery proceedings help to assure that all sides have had access to evidence, and that records of observations of the evidence will be preserved, even if the evidence itself decays or disappears before trial. Discovery may also encourage the preservation of evidence that otherwise might be allowed to change or be destroyed.

As useful as discovery is for expediting the work of the courts, legislators have not wished to tamper with the traditional adversary nature of the trial in court, nor to allow attorneys to use discovery to take unfair advantage of their opponents. Consequently, there are some types of information that are considered privileged and thus not subject to discovery. The types of privileged information most relevant to product failure cases are privileged communication between attorney and client, and the "work product" of the attorney. The expert consultant's work may fall into one or the other of these categories under certain circumstances.

Communication between you and the attorney will not ordinarily be considered privileged. Only in a few instances, such as when you must act as intermediary between the client and the attorney, can your communication with the attorney be regarded as privileged. This could happen, for instance, when the client cannot directly and adequately communicate certain information to the attorney because of insufficient technical knowledge. In general, you should assume that your communication with the attorney is not privileged.

The work product doctrine is more likely to affect you. This doctrine is intended to protect the privacy of the attorney's preparation of the case, in order to allow full investigation of all aspects of the case without prejudice. The question of how much of the expert consultant's work can be considered part of the attorney's investigation is often at issue. A rule of thumb that applies in most but not all cases is that the contributions of a consultant are not subject to discovery until the consultant has been designated as a witness. Where there is disagreement on this question, the final decision is up to the court.

PROFESSIONAL PUBLICATIONS, INC.   Belmont, CA

DISCOVERY AND THE EXPERT WITNESS
Up to this point we have been considering discovery essentially from the point of view of the court. Let us now look at the implications of discovery for the expert witness.

Before designation by the attorney as a potential witness at trial, the work of the expert is not usually subject to discovery. However, after designation, the expert may expect to encounter several instruments of discovery, including the interrogatory, the subpoena, and the deposition.

The Interrogatory. The interrogatory is a device for obtaining written information from witnesses. It consists of a list of questions drawn up by opposing counsel. Rather than giving your answers directly to opposing counsel, however, you will give your answers to the attorney who has retained you. The attorney will edit your answers and cast them into the customary form, then return them to you for corrections. After corrections, the document will be notarized and submitted to opposing counsel. Your answers to the interrogatory are admissible in court, and may be used, like any other part of your testimony, in the attempt to impeach your credibility.

The attorney who has retained you may ask for your assistance in preparing questions for interrogatories for the expert or other witnesses engaged by the opposition. This will serve the dual purpose of obtaining information from the other side, and helping to inform the attorney with whom you are working about some of the technical aspects of the case.

The Subpoena. A subpoena is a written order directing you to appear at a particular time and place to testify as a witness. While a subpoena is often used to compel the attendance of a witness in court, it may also be used to compel a person to testify in pretrial proceedings, such as depositions, as well. The subpoena may be issued by the court, or it may be issued directly by the attorney of record in any action pending before the court. Your first subpoena will probably be one requiring you to appear for a deposition, and it will probably be issued and signed by the attorney for the opposition.

For the subpoena to be effective, it must be delivered to you personally, usually by a process server. If you so request, the person delivering the subpoena must pay you a fee for travel to and from the place at which your attendance is required (in the case of a deposition, usually the office of one of the attorneys), and a fee for one day's attendance there. These fees are set by statute, and may vary by state and by year. However, many state codes also allow the expert witness to charge opposition counsel a fee "not exceeding his or her customary hourly or daily fee." Each state may have different rates and different regulations.

The subpoena has the force of a court order, and failure to obey a subpoena may be punished as contempt of court. A person found in contempt of court may be fined or even jailed.

If you receive a subpoena, you should immediately notify the attorney by whom you have been retained. If for some reason it will be difficult for you to appear at the time and place specified in the subpoena, the attorney for whom you are consulting can probably arrange with the attorney who has subpoenaed you a mutually agreeable time and place to meet. In fact, it is possible for the two attorneys to settle such arrangements in advance, so that the subpoena reflects your preferences in the matter. On occasion, it is possible simply to arrange an appointment that is suitable for all parties, eliminating the need for a subpoena. Whatever the arrangements may be, you should not attempt to deal directly with the opposing counsel, but work through the attorney who has engaged you.

You may receive a *subpoena duces tecum,* which requires not only your attendance and testimony, but also requires you to bring with you specified materials. These may include books, notes, other documents, or any relevant item in your possession or under your control. In order to be effective, this type of subpoena must be accompanied by an affidavit which designates exactly what items must be produced, and shows good cause for requiring them. That is, it must show that the items being requested have a material bearing on the case, and also that they are in your possession or under your control.

With this type of subpoena, the opposition attorney will probably be trying to obtain everything that you may have used to arrive at the opinion that you plan to give in the deposition. That means that copies of any books or articles that you have written on relevant subjects, as well as your working file on the case, will almost certainly be requested.

You may have doubts about the material being requested. For instance, it may seem to you that some of the material is not germane to the case, or you may feel that such a large amount of material is being requested that assembling it would be very troublesome. Or you may suspect that some of what is being requested should be regarded as confidential or privileged material.

If you have any doubts of this sort, you should discuss them with the attorney who has retained you. The attorney may be able to negotiate a smaller volume of material, or to determine whether any of the material is privileged and not subject to discovery, or, if necessary, to get a protective order from the court. It is prudent to discuss any subpoena with the attorney when you receive it, whether or not you perceive any problems with it.

The Deposition. A deposition is a statement made under oath in response to questioning by an attorney. Although the witness testifies under oath, the procedures governing depositions are relatively informal compared to those of the courtroom. Not only the attorney taking the deposition, but attorneys for all parties to the litigation may be present and ask questions. The proceedings will be recorded by a certified legal stenographer, who will also prepare a transcript of the deposition. This transcript may be used during the trial.

The deposition is a basic tool of the discovery process, and you should expect to have to give a deposition in virtually every case for which you serve as an expert witness. No lawyer wants to be surprised in court with damaging evidence or expert testimony, and a competent attorney will try to prepare for trial by gathering all possible information, including information on the investigation and opinions of the expert witness retained by opposing counsel. Therefore it will be to your benefit, as an expert witness, to be informed about the deposition process, and to prepare carefully for your role as deponent.

The information obtained by taking the deposition of the expert witness serves several purposes for the attorney for the opposition. First, the attorney must evaluate the relative merits of the evidence and arguments that will be advanced by both sides in order to decide whether or not to try to settle out of court. (If this point seems to be overemphasized, remember that only about ten per cent of these types of cases actually go to court, and that the decision to persist through a trial is often a very costly one for both sides.) If the opinions you express in your deposition, and the evidence on which you base them, seem well-founded, the attorney may try to convince the client to seek a settlement before trial.

However, this is not the only possible outcome. Occasionally, a client will insist on a trial as a matter of principle, or more often, the two sides will not be able to agree on the amount of settlement. When this happens, the trial may be used more for establishing the amount of settlement than for determining responsibility for the failure incident. Your pretrial testimony may encourage an out-of-court settlement, but it may also fail to do so.

The opposing counsel is likely to have engaged an expert witness, who will probably be present at your deposition to advise the attorney on lines of questioning and on the soundness of your conclusions. (Likewise, you may be requested to attend the deposition given by the other expert, and to advise the attorney who has retained you.) With or without the assistance of the expert, the attorney may become convinced that your testimony, although it appears to be damaging, can be successfully challenged on logical or other grounds.

Since the deposition can be quoted from in court, the attorney may attempt to catch you in ambiguities or self-contradictions which can then be used to undermine the credibility of your courtroom testimony during cross-examination. The second major purpose of the deposition, then, is to serve as a guide to the opposition counsel in preparing a strategy for questioning and argument during the trial.

The Pre-Deposition Conference. Because the deposition you give can be used in court, and certainly will provide the opposing counsel with ideas about how to conduct the trial, you should prepare yourself carefully before the deposition. As soon as the date of your deposition is set, the attorney who has retained you will almost certainly want to schedule a pre-deposition conference.

This conference can and should be beneficial to both you and the attorney. You can maximize the benefit to both of you if you prepare adequately ahead of time. Review your investigation and conclusions, so that you come to the conference with a clear grasp of what you believe the facts of the case to be. It is also important to come to the conference with an open mind, willing to learn what the attorney has to teach you.

Throughout your work on a case, you will find that an important part of your working relationship with the attorney is a kind of mutual education. Each of you has a different field of specialization, with its professional language, jargon, and techniques. For your part, you will need to communicate enough about the principles involved in the incident you are investigating to enable the attorney to ask the appropriate questions and advance the appropriate arguments during the trial. The attorney, in turn, will need to give you enough information about legal procedures to enable you to function effectively as a witness.

Even after you have acquired some experience in the courtroom, you will find that the technicalities of each case are different, and you will continue to need some guidance from the attorney. While your consultation during the investigation phase will probably have provided some of this mutual education, it is likely that the pre-deposition conference will give both of you the fullest opportunity to arrive at a satisfactory mutual understanding of what the case is all about.

The attorney will have two major aims in the pre-deposition conference. The first will be to ensure a full understanding of your opinions and their bases before you reveal them to opposing counsel. The second will be to help you to give the most effective testimony possible by preparing you for what to expect during the deposition proceedings.

This preparation usually consists of three elements. First, the attorney will try to help you anticipate the kinds of questions you are likely to be asked by opposing counsel. It is important not to be taken by surprise, because any hesitation or apparent confusion on your part during the deposition, particularly if the question seems to be a fundamental one, may be used during the trial to undermine your credibility with the jury. Your previous consideration during the investigation phase of all possible hypotheses, along with the attorney's suggestions, will help to reduce the possibility of such embarrassment.

The attorney, in addition to trying to anticipate the questions likely to be asked by opposing counsel, will probably offer advice on how to deal with these questions. For instance, you will probably be shown how to avoid giving more information than the question actually asks for, and how to respond to a question that rests on dubious logical assumptions. It is important to learn to avoid the traps that can be set by a clever attorney.

You should beware, however, of suggestions that you alter your testimony in any way. Your testimony should reflect only the facts and your true opinions based on your investigation and knowledge. Perjury is a crime punishable by law. Any suggestion that you perjure yourself, even by a slight shading of your testimony, should be immediately and emphatically rejected.

Giving a Deposition. Attorneys for all parties to a litigation may be present at a deposition, and they may question the witness. Ordinarily, the attorney who is taking the deposition will conduct a direct examination, which is followed by cross-examination by the attorney who has retained you and any other attorneys for interested parties who may be present. This is the reverse of the usual procedure in court, where the direct examination is conducted by "friendly" counsel and the cross-examination is conducted by the counsel for the opposition.

A deposition given by an expert witness marks a critical juncture in the preparation of a case for trial. The deposition will make clear to all parties what to expect from the expert during trial, both in terms of information and opinion and in terms of demeanor and image. Both of these are of potentially great importance in determining the outcome of a trial, or in deciding whether to go to court. Because of the significance of the deposition, you should approach a deposition just as carefully as you approach actual testimony in court.

The deposition will represent the opposition attorney's first opportunity to gain full access to your findings and opinions. You will probably be questioned closely about your investigation, including the observations you made, the methods you used, the conclusions you reached, and the principles you used in reaching those conclusions. The attorney may have retained an expert consultant. If so, the consultant will probably advise the attorney on lines of questioning, and you may find yourself being confronted with surprisingly sophisticated questions. Your previous consideration of all possible hypotheses will stand you in good stead during questioning.

Particularly if your professional opinion appears to be a sound one, the opposition attorney may try many tactics to undermine your credibility. One means of discrediting you may be to question your qualifications as an expert in the particular case, and so your educational background and experience may be closely examined. A second way to try to discredit you is to catch ambiguities or contradictions in your testimony.

If you are adequately prepared for testifying, you will have anticipated many of the questions, and your testimony will probably be largely free of self-contradictory or fuzzy statements. However, the opposition attorney's style of questioning may be specifically designed to elicit unclear or contradictory responses.

A common tactic is for the opposition attorney to ask, "What are your opinions in this case?" If you answer the question as stated, it may later be held that your answer constitutes the whole of your opinions in the case. If anything you forgot or left out should come up in the trial later, the answer may be objected to on the grounds that such an opinion was not given during discovery procedures. While it is not likely, you could even be accused of perjury for failing to give all pertinent information during the deposition. Rather than answering such a question in its stated form, it is better to say that you have many opinions on the case, and to ask the attorney to specify which aspect of the case you should give your opinion on.

If a question is unclear, or if it rests on unclear or incorrect assumptions, you should say that the question is ambiguous and cannot be answered as it stands. If a question is virtually the same as a previous question, refer to your previous response to that question. Where possible, refer to your written report for answers. This will help to minimize inconsistencies and to focus the line of questioning. If you are not sure of the answer to a question, it is better to decline to give an opinion than to try to make up something plausible. Rarely, a question will bring up a problem that you have not anticipated at all. In this case, it is best to say that the question requires further investigation.

At some points during the deposition, the attorney who has retained you may object to a question. Usually you will answer such a question anyway, and the attorney's objection will be a part of the record. If a question seems improper to you, but the attorney does not raise an objection, you may request a recess for a brief conference. Obviously, too many such requests could create a negative impression, but if you are genuinely troubled by a question or line of questioning, you should not hesitate to ask for a short recess. Occasionally, you may be instructed not to answer a question, and you should follow this instruction.

At all times during testimony, it is best to limit your answers to the question at hand. If you give unnecessary information or opinions, you provide the opposition attorney with extra opportunities to try to trip you up. You may feel that you are not being allowed to state your opinions fully. Nevertheless, you should resist the temptation to expand on your answers. You will get an opportunity to give the information you wish to give, as the attorney who has retained you will question you in such a way as to allow you to present your findings and opinions in a coherent and orderly fashion.

Uses of the Deposition. The transcript of a deposition constitutes a document which may be used at trial. The deposition is recorded by a legal stenographer and is later transcribed in typewritten form. When the transcription is completed, the court reporter will notify the parties that it is available for reading and correcting. If no other arrangements are made, it will be necessary to go to the office of the court reporter to read and correct the document. However, if agreed to by all parties present at the deposition, it is possible for you to be provided with a copy of the transcript and for you to forward corrections through the attorney who has retained you.

In either case, corrections must be made and the document signed within 30 days after notification. If not signed within 30 days, it will be considered that you have waived your right to make changes. The deposition can then be used in court in exactly the same way as if it had been corrected and signed. You can also voluntarily waive your reading of the deposition, but this is a risky decision. Without reading the transcript, you have no way of knowing what errors are in this document which can be used, and used against you, in court.

A deposition can be used as direct evidence in court if the witness cannot be present because of illness or other conditions which make it impossible to compel his or her attendance. In such a situation, the deposition is simply read into the court record as if the deponent were actually testifying.

A much more likely use of the deposition is to impeach (call into question) the credibility of the expert. Since this is an almost routine procedure, you may expect your deposition to be used for this purpose. Most commonly, the opposition attorney will point out discrepancies between your courtroom testimony and your deposition, and use such discrepancies to shake the jury's faith in your credibility.

What Are Depositions For?[*] All Federal and most state courts follow what are known as the Rules of Civil Procedure. First adopted by the United States Supreme Court in 1938 and amended from time to time since then, the Rules govern how lawyers prepare and try civil cases.

Rule 26 provides for different "discovery methods," including depositions. The purpose of "discovery" is to obtain information from the opposing party in advance of the trial to avoid surprise and to promote settlements. The theory is that once litigants know how strong or weak their (or their opponent's) case is the more likely it is they will arrive at a fair settlement. Further, by eliminating surprise at the trial, each side can properly prepare, with appropriate rebuttal witnesses if necessary, for a trial on all issues of merit.

---

[*] The material in this section is reprinted from *Johnson's Guide For Witnesses*, published by Law Forum Press, Seattle, Washington.

Your Rights as a Witness. In terms of depositions, a potential witness is anyone who has information that may lead to relevant information. Civil Rule 26(b) gives depositions a broader scope of inquiry than would be possible at trial. Unlike at a trial, where a judge can rule on objections according to established rules of evidence, at a deposition lawyers can ask irrelevant questions and inquire into hearsay.

Rule 26 specifically states that it "is not ground for objection that the information sought will be inadmissible at the trial if the information sought appears reasonably calculated to lead to the discovery of admissible evidence."

This "fishing expedition" aspect of depositions can justify inquiries into areas sensitive to you that have nothing to do with the lawsuit. Lawyers in the case may even decide to sue you after your deposition, on the basis of your testimony, to make you an additional party to their lawsuit.

Even if your deposition deals with innocuous facts, you may be unduly inconvenienced in your job and home life unless you are aware of your rights.

A call to your lawyer before your deposition can save a great deal of unpleasantness. Tell him what you know about the case, the names of others involved, and the name of the lawyer who wants to depose you. Be completely frank with him; what you discuss cannot be forced out of you at your deposition, since it is protected by the attorney-client privilege. Based on what you tell him, he may decide to be at your deposition with you to protect your rights, or he may counsel you to call him at any time during the deposition.

Whether your lawyer is subpoenaed or volunteers to appear at your deposition, you will have to pay your own attorney's fees.

If your lawyer is an experienced trial attorney, he knows the general reputation of the lawyer or lawyers seeking your deposition. If they are "straight shooters," in his opinion, you probably can relax.

Your lawyer also knows the peculiar local customs, practices, and laws of your jurisdiction. Trust his advice on the specifics of your case.

Rights Generally Applicable. In most instances, your lawyer will confirm that you have the following rights in a deposition.

- the right not to incriminate yourself

If you feel any answer you give at a deposition may ultimately provide information that could put you behind bars, have a lawyer present at your deposition. If you start answering any line of potentially incriminating questions, you may be deemed to have waived your Fifth Amendment right to silence. At that point you have blown it—there is no way to put the toothpaste back into the tube.

You do not need a lawyer present, however, to invoke the privilege. Say: "I refuse to answer that question as it might tend to incriminate me," or words to that effect.

In civil cases, a lawyer hostile to your side can call to the jury's attention the fact that you "took the Fifth" and can suggest conclusions about why you did so. Thus, "taking the Fifth" can have serious consequences, and it is foolish to do so if it is not necessary. Again, follow the advice of a trained and experienced lawyer.

- the right to the attorney-client privilege

Anything you discuss with your own lawyer is "out of bounds" in a deposition. It is your privilege, and you may invoke it by stating: "That question asks me to divulge communications between me and my lawyer, and I invoke the attorney-client privilege in not answering that question," or words to that effect.

If you think you might be wrong to invoke the privilege, ask for a break while you discuss the matter with your lawyer. (If any lawyer present refuses your request, take the break anyway. You are nobody's chattel at your deposition, and unless your behavior is intentionally disruptive, so that a judge orders you to sit still, you are free to move about and take breaks as you like.)

The attorney-client privilege is lost if your conversations with your lawyer take place in the presence of third parties, such as your friends or your spouse. There is an exception to this rule if the third parties have a "community of interest" with you in a given matter, but why risk losing the privilege if you can help it?

There is also no attorney-client privilege between you and a lawyer who is not your lawyer. Your company's lawyer can be considered "your" lawyer if your discussions relate to matters of your employment with the company, or if that attorney customarily handles employees' personal legal problems as part of his duties. But your company's lawyer may have a potential conflict of interest if he or she ever has to represent both the company and you in any given matter. It's always best to have your own lawyer advise you, even if it costs more in the short run because in the long run it may cost much more to act on your own.

The attorney-client privilege, like the Fifth Amendment rights, can be waived if at any time you start to talk about what you and your lawyer discussed. An interrogator may ask innocuous questions about your dealings with your lawyer just to get you in a position where you will waive the privilege.

If you have had significant conversations with your lawyer about anything dealing with the case, the best protection against inadvertently waiving your attorney-client privilege is to have your lawyer with you at the deposition.

- the right to a subpoena

The only way you can be forced to give a deposition is through the service of a subpoena upon you personally. You are usually also entitled to a modest witness fee, which should accompany the subpoena, calculated on the basis of how far you will have to travel to your deposition. If you are entitled to a witness fee and do not get one in advance of the deposition, you can ignore the subpoena.

Unfortunately, unless you are an expert witness hired to give testimony for a party, you are not entitled to compensation for lost wages of business opportunities during the time of your deposition. You are performing a civic duty.

You cannot be subpoenaed to a deposition far from where you live. The subpoena power of courts varies, but as a general rule you cannot be subpoenaed to appear at a deposition outside of the county where you live (for most state lawsuits) or outside the jurisdictional boundaries of the U.S. District Court where you reside. This may encompass part or all of your state, but not more (the districts do not cross state borders). Thus, it may be possible to avoid your deposition altogether if the lawyer requesting it does not wish to bear the expense of travelling to your state.

It is generally a good idea to insist on a subpoena, even if it is a hassle for the lawyer wanting your testimony on the record, especially if you are expected to produce documents that you or others consider confidential or sensitive.

* the right to a protective order

You have the right to a protective order to keep records confidential; to guard trade secrets; to limit the scope of discovery; to limit the number of persons present at your deposition; to foreclose discovery altogether; or to limit discovery to some method other than deposition.

Rule 26(c) provides for judicial intervention in any of the above circumstances, before your deposition begins. If you are entrusted with confidential information or have reason to believe that your deposition is to promote chicanery, have your lawyer seek a protective order forbidding any undesirable acts before they happen.

Experience has shown that courts are willing to protect trade secrets from disclosure, but otherwise allow the free flow of unbridled depositions, regardless of the inconvenience to the witness.

* the right to bring anything that may assist you

If you want to bring this book as a handy reference guide, go ahead and do so.

If you, or others, have prepared notes that will help your recollection, bring them (but expect them to be made exhibits). Don't, however, bring rehearsed, "pat" answers to anticipated questions. That will severely hurt your credibility, since most people associate truth-telling with ease and spontaneity of response.

Other items may be helpful, depending on the type of case and the testimony you anticipate giving, such as rulers (to make schematic or scaled drawings), a calendar, a calculator, or maps.

If you are the victim of injuries and will testify about your pain and suffering, it is a good idea (unless there is contrary advice from your lawyer) to keep a diary of how you feel each day and the dosages of any medications you are taking. Such a chronicle can be indispensable at the time of your deposition or trial months or years later, when you have healed and look the picture of health.

Bring a thermos of tea or juice if you don't like coffee (the standard deposition beverage).

- the right not to answer a question

Only a judge can order you to answer a question, but be sure you have a good reason for a refusal to answer. Repeated refusals on frivolous grounds can result in your being held in contempt, with attendant fines or jail until you do answer.

Always refuse to answer if your attorney so instructs you.

- the right to change an answer after the deposition

Rule 30(e) gives you the right to read your deposition, once it is transcribed, and make any corrections, such as of typos or misspellings. Too often, however, lawyers, perhaps unaware of this rule, mistakenly tell witnesses they may correct for typos and misspellings only. More important, you can even change your answers if you feel they were wrong or incomplete. State the reason for each change. Then sign the deposition, and all your changes are tacked on as an addendum to the official transcript.

You will most likely be questioned thoroughly at the trial about any substantial changes in the transcript. Be prepared for these questions, and be open and forthright in defending the changes. Be quick to admit a mistake, which will aid your credibility.

At the end of your deposition, one or more interrogators may suggest that you "waive signature." This means you will thereby be giving up your right to read the final transcript and make corrections. Often this can be a convenience to the witness if the deposition is of no consequence. But if your deposition might have any significance at all, do not fall for the invitation to "waive signature" as a supposed courtesy to you. One of the interrogators may mislead you into thinking that reading your testimony will only bore you, and all you will do is correct occasional typos, anyway. They rarely tell you that you will also have the opportunity to make any changes you wish regarding your testimony!

A court reporter says about many lawyers' apparent ignorance of Rule 30(e):

"Almost always, when discussing signature, lawyers tell the witnesses they can't make substantive changes in testimony, but can only correct the court reporter. I have seen this done countless times. It's amazing that so many lawyers don't know about Rule 30.

"Whenever I can, I try to beat these lawyers to it by saying to the witness something like 'Where can I notify you that the transcript is ready to be read, corrected, and signed?' The reporter has to jump right in there, as soon as the last attorney says, 'Well, looks like that's it,' or someone will start the old 'can't-make-changes' speech.

"I must have bitten my tongue a thousand times so as not to correct some well-intentioned but uninformed lawyer giving this erroneous advice. I've wanted, for years, to have my people carry a copy of Rule 30(e) to hand to the witness at the end of the deposition, but have been too chicken."

Even if all you do is correct typos, that is reason enough to go over your transcribed testimony. Court reporters are not infallible and may have unintentionally put words in your mouth. Further, a word spoken by you may be ambiguous when looked at in the cold record. When you are given a finished, typed copy of the transcript to review, you have a golden opportunity to set the record straight with whatever additional words you want to add.

The deposition can be used to "impeach" you at trial, which means a lawyer may produce a copy of your deposition and ask you to read along with him specified questions he asked and the answers you gave. His intent will be to show an inconsistency between your deposition testimony and trial testimony. If your deposition testimony is harmful to an interrogator's case, he will look for every opportunity to make you look like a liar or a fool before the jury. By not "waiving signature," you minimize the potential occurrence of those opportunities.

- other rights

You will usually have additional rights as well, such as the following:

- If you have given a prior statement, you are entitled to a copy of it.

- If you are asked through the subpoena process to bring documents with you, you may retain the originals and supply copies. However, bring both the originals and the copies to the deposition to allow the opposing attorney to compare the two.

- You may limit the duration of your deposition. Your attorney can end a long deposition if he can show that the questioning is conducted in bad faith or in such a manner as to unreasonably annoy, embarrass, or oppress you.

- You can ask for a break at any time during a deposition. If it is not granted, you may take it anyway.

CREDIBILITY AS A DEPONENT

One of the most important reasons for engaging you as an expert witness is to take advantage of your credibility. What determines your credibility or believability as a witness?

First of all, expertise is directly related to credibility. If you have specialized experience in the type of problem that is at hand, and especially if you have written papers or books treating that type of problem, you will have greater credibility than someone without such experience. The attorney for the opposition will probably question you in detail about your qualifications as an expert in the particular case, from your education to your experience to your scholarly work.

The attorney will use this information to compare your qualifications with those of the expert who may have been retained by the other side. If your credentials are more impressive, the opposition may be more inclined to seek an out-of-court settlement. On the other hand, if the other expert appears to be better qualified, or if the two of you do not differ greatly in qualifications, the opposition may be encouraged in going to court.

Whether or not the opposition has engaged an expert witness, the attorney will probably seek information about your professional qualifications which would cast doubt on your expertise in the particular case, thereby reducing your credibility. Therefore, it is advisable to go to the deposition prepared to explain clearly why you should be considered an expert with regard to the problem in question in the case.

Lack of any material interest in the outcome of the case is a second factor affecting an expert's credibility. It goes without saying that you will not take any case which involves an actual conflict of interest. However, in order to preserve your credibility, you should also avoid all cases which may involve even a remote appearance of conflict of interest. Ordinarily, you will have taken all precautions regarding possible conflict of interest long before the deposition. Nevertheless, you should be prepared to be questioned on your connections with any and all parties to the litigation, and on any other matter that may pertain to your interest in the case.

The third factor affecting credibility is your behavior or demeanor as a witness. The first two factors, expertise and disinterest, can only be reported on, but your behavior can be directly observed. Your demeanor may be extremely influential on judgments of your credibility. Lack of expert qualifications or suspicions of conflict of interest probably cannot be overcome by a convincing performance, but the credibility established by excellent credentials can be destroyed by a poor performance. Your success as a forensic engineer will depend in large part on your development of skills in testifying effectively, both as a deponent and as a witness in court.

There are several components involved in effective performance as a witness. They include manner of dress, language, gestures, and all other cues that observers use to judge another person's self-presentation.

The most important rule to remember is to make all of your behavior consistent with your status as expert. That is, you should behave as an expert is expected to behave. An overall consistent performance is more important in creating a credible image than any of the elements taken alone. In order to present a consistent image, however, you must pay attention to the details that contribute to the image.

Your style of dress is one of the first things that the opposition attorney

PROFESSIONAL PUBLICATIONS, INC.   Belmont, CA

will notice about you. It is best to choose conservative clothing—preferably a dark suit, white shirt, and tie if you are a man, or a dark suit and conservative blouse if you are a woman. Pay attention to details, such as carrying a professional-looking attache case, having your shoes shined, and having your hair neatly combed.

Many engineers dress more casually in their day-to-day work, and you may feel uncomfortable in what you may regard as a business uniform. Forensic engineering, however, will require this uniform on occasion, and you should wear it often enough to feel comfortable and at ease while wearing it. If you feel awkward or ill at ease in your clothes, it will make you to some degree a less effective witness. If you fail to dress appropriately, you will not look the part of an expert, and accordingly you may lose some of your credibility.

Just as your clothes ought to look appropriate for an expert, so should your bearing, gestures, and tone of voice suit your expert role. An erect but relaxed posture will convey a sense of authority; slouching or sprawling in your seat will convey the opposite. Gestures should be restrained but appear natural. Quick, nervous movements, expansive arm-waving, or pointing with a finger or pencil are all distracting to the observer, and may result in a lowered estimation of your credibility.

Especially when giving a deposition, be careful not to let gestures carry any of the essential meaning of what you are trying to say. Only your words will be recorded, not your gestures. This means, for instance, that a nod, a shake of the head, or a shrug, each carrying very different meanings, will all go into the record simply as silence, while the little wink that tells an observer not to take seriously what is being said will not be there for the reader of the transcript. Answers in which you have relied on gestures to get across part of your meaning can come back to haunt you most embarrassingly during the trial.

Like your gestures, your tone of voice should reflect calm and restraint. In taking depositions, some attorneys behave very politely, but some may badger and challenge the witness. If you are faced with the second type, it is crucial not to let yourself get riled. If you reply in an argumentative tone, or begin to raise your voice, you will give the attorney ammunition for the attack on your credibility in court. If you begin to argue or show anger, you will seem more like an advocate of a position than an objective expert. You should also avoid using a mocking or sarcastic tone. Such a tone would imply that you do not take the proceedings seriously. In turn, you may not be taken seriously.

It is also important to speak clearly. If you mumble, or if your voice is inaudible, you will give the impression that you are not sure of yourself, or even that you do not know what you are talking about. You should speak loudly enough to be heard by all participants, and you should enunciate your words clearly.

One of the most critical elements in your expert image is your use of language. Effective use of language will greatly strengthen your position as expert, and inept language use can weaken it disastrously.

The most basic requirement is correct grammar. Few college graduates fail to use the correct pronouns or make mistakes in conjugating common verbs. However, a surprising number are careless about mixing singular and plural noun and verb forms in complex sentences, make vague references, and leave many sentences incomplete. Such mistakes are easy to make and may even be inevitable when you have to think on your feet. Nonetheless, they make a poor impression on the listener, who is at more leisure to think about the fine points of sentence construction while you are struggling to put your thoughts into words.

Remember that the deposition will be recorded in written form, and that grammatical errors are much more glaring in writing. Slang expressions and responses such as "uh-huh" and "yeah" also make a poor impression in a written transcript.

When you are giving narrative answers, use complete sentences insofar as possible. Fillers such as "ah," "uh," or "you know" are distracting to the listener and make you seem unsure of what you are saying. A thorough review of your material in the days just before the deposition will help you to seem more fluent and articulate.

Although you will boost your credibility by being fluent and articulate in your speech, you can lower it by being too talkative. A verbose witness may seem to be trying to make up for lack of knowledge or solid evidence. Talking too much also carries the danger of straying from the subject of the question and giving unnecessary information.

Forensic experts have found that style of speech is also an important element in credibility. They suggest that the same information can be communicated in either powerful language or powerless language, but it will be more convincing when couched in powerful language. Answers using powerful language are short but complete, clear, specific, and decisive. Answers using powerless language may be overly long, incomplete, fuzzy, and hesitant. A few examples may illustrate the difference.

PROFESSIONAL PUBLICATIONS, INC.   Belmont, CA

Powerful	Powerless
Yes.	Uh, I guess so.
Thirty minutes.	It must have been a half an hour or so.
It could support a load of 750 pounds.	It could support a pretty large load, uh, you know, about seven or eight hundred pounds.

Using powerful language will make you appear more knowledgeable, more self-confident, and better prepared—in short, it will make you seem more expert. Using powerless language will have the opposite effect, making you seem less sure of your knowledge and opinions. There are less obvious effects as well. Research on the effect of language shows that powerful language also makes the witness seem more truthful, intelligent, and trustworthy. If you devote much of your time to forensic engineering, the use of powerful language is an important skill to acquire or develop.

TESTIFYING IN COURT

Preparing to Testify. After depositions are taken by attorneys for both parties to a litigation, there will follow a period of waiting for the date of trial. Although further negotiation may go on between the contesting parties, and the attorneys may continue to work on their preparations for trial, as an expert witness you may have nothing further to do with the case until just before the trial begins.

Shortly before the trial date, you will probably be invited to a meeting with the attorney who retained you to go over the testimony you will give. Before this meeting, you should review your investigation and any theoretical work you may have done to form your opinion. It will be helpful to review your answers to interrogatories and your deposition. Study the parts of depositions given by other experts and witnesses that relate to the subject of your testimony.

Your conference with the attorney may resemble the pre-deposition conference in some respects. You will go over the facts and opinions that you intend to present, and try to anticipate the types of questions that may come up in cross-examination. The attorney will probably try to prepare you for what to expect in the courtroom. Much of the advice and information will be similar to that you received in the pre-deposition conference. However, courtroom procedure is much more formal than the procedure in the taking of a deposition, and much more rigidly regulated by rules and traditions. You will need to know the sequence of events in courtroom examination, and the rules that govern your behavior as a witness. You may try to anticipate the approach and style that will be used by the attorney for the opposition.

Most important, together you will draw up a plan for the direct examination (courtroom examination by the attorney who has engaged you). Particularly if the case is a complex one, this process may be quite time-consuming. It is important to consider all the facts of the case, as well as the order in which these facts should be presented to give the most coherent, comprehensible, and persuasive support to your expert opinion. All possible alternative explanations of the facts should be considered, along with ways of rebutting those explanations which are contrary to your opinion. If there are other technical experts working on the case, your testimony should be coordinated with theirs. Rely on the lawyer to bring out your evidence and theirs in a coordinated manner.

Since you will not have witnessed the incident in question, you will be obliged to reconstruct it in response to hypothetical questions posed by the attorney. The assumptions of the hypothetical question must be supported by the factual evidence of the case. Your work with the attorney in structuring the content and sequence of questioning will be of fundamental importance in the success of your testimony.

In general, it is best to limit presentation of the facts to those which have an actual bearing on your opinion. Too many facts which are not essential to your opinion will only confuse the jury, and provide targets for attacks by opposing counsel. A smaller number of facts and assumptions usually make for a tighter and more coherent argument.

On the other hand, it can be fatal to your argument to omit any of the necessary facts. To guard against any such crucial omissions, it is advisable to write out in full the questions and answers that you jointly agree should constitute the direct examination.

A written text provides you with an excellent means of checking whether the presentation is complete and logically convincing. As you study it, you can make corrections and look for likely points of attack during cross-examination. In addition, the final text will be helpful for your review immediately prior to being called to testify. It will also help to insure that the attorney asks all the necessary questions, and in the appropriate sequence.

PROFESSIONAL PUBLICATIONS, INC.   Belmont, CA

Some attorneys may not allocate enough time for a satisfactory pretrial conference. There are even stories of last-minute words of advice delivered in the courthouse corridors just before the expert is called to the witness stand. Obviously, this is far from the ideal situation. If it should happen to you, your only recourse is to prepare yourself without the assistance of the attorney. In such a situation, review all your previous work and pay special attention to the transcript of your deposition.

Before Testimony. When the trial begins, the moment for which you have been preparing for so long will finally have arrived: you will be called to testify in court, before a judge and jury. In order to avoid delays, you will probably be summoned to the court sometime before the attorney anticipates that you will actually be called to the witness stand. In order to avoid unnecessary expense, you will be summoned as close as possible to the time you will be called.

You are not expected to be present throughout the trial, although the attorney who has engaged you may wish to consult with you about points that come up in phases of the trial other than your testimony. Do not come to court unless you are requested to do so. Your continuous presence could imply that you have something other than an expert's interest in the progress and outcome of the trial.

When you arrive at the courthouse, be careful not to discuss the case or your role in it with anyone other than the attorney who has engaged you. Be courteous but cautious with everyone you meet. The pleasant (or obnoxious) person that you encounter in the corridor could turn out to be one of the jurors. Also, counsel for the opposition may have posted clerks in various locations around the courtroom. Your overheard conversation could be used to damage your credibility during cross-examination.

You should behave in a restrained manner toward the expert(s) engaged by the opposition, even if you are well-acquainted with one another, regard one another as respected colleagues, or are friends. An effusive greeting, if witnessed by any of the jurors, may raise the credibility of the other expert. Under no circumstances should you discuss the case with the opposition expert. Do not feel rebuffed by the coolness of the other expert, who is operating under the same restrictions.

Particularly if it is your first time in court, you will probably feel somewhat anxious. Some degree of "pretrial jitters" is normal, even for a seasoned forensic engineer. The best way to allay your anxiety is to be as fully informed and prepared as possible.

Stages of the Examination. What can you expect while on the witness stand? First, you will be directly examined and cross-examined on your background and experience. Following this examination, the trial judge will rule on your qualifications as an expert witness. Then you will be directly examined by the attorney who has called you as a witness. After direct examination, you will be cross-examined by the opposition attorney. A second round of redirect examination and recross-examination may be called for to clarify points that came up in the initial examinations. You will then be excused from the witness stand. Let us look at each of these stages in the examination in more detail.

Establishing Qualification as an Expert. Before you are called to the witness stand, the need for expert testimony will have been established to the court's satisfaction. Following your testimony regarding your qualifications, the judge will rule that you may or may not testify as a witness. A ruling allowing you to testify must be made before you can testify regarding your opinions in the case.

In ruling on whether you will be allowed to testify, the judge is obliged to consider your qualifications against certain criteria. An expert is considered to be a person who has knowledge, skills, education, training, or experience not available to the average person. In addition, the expertise must relate directly and specifically to the subject on which an opinion must be rendered.

In order to establish your qualifications, the attorney who is calling you as a witness will directly examine you. You will be asked to detail your education and experience as they relate to the question at hand. If you have written books or articles on the subject, you will be asked about them.

Following the presentation of your credentials in direct examination, the counsel for the opposition will be allowed to cross-examine you on your qualifications. If there is any way to challenge the relevance of your expertise to the subject, the opposition attorney will pursue it. If sufficient doubt can be raised regarding your qualifications, the judge may rule that you cannot testify as an expert witness. If you have been careful to accept a case only when it is clearly within your competence, any challenge by the opposition attorney will probably fail.

You can facilitate the proceedings by providing a resume which sets out your education, training, experience, and accomplishments (e.g., publications) as they relate to the subject in question. Both attorneys may waive questioning if the resume contains all the necessary information, or if the applicability of your expertise seems indisputable.

In any case, the decision is within the judge's discretion. If the judge rules that you may testify as an expert witness, it is unlikely that the ruling will be overturned through appeal.

Rules of Evidence. When your qualifications have been approved, you will be examined and cross-examined. The core of your testimony will be your opinion and the basis on which you arrived at it. While testifying, you should be mindful of the fact that there are legal limitations on what you may say in support of your opinion.

The first rule for lay witnesses is that the matter in question must be personally known to you. That is, you must have actually witnessed the event in question. This rule is broadened for expert witnesses, so that the only requirement is that the matter must have been made known to you at or before the hearing at which you give your opinion. The fact that you have inspected the physical or other types of evidence will help to establish your knowledge of the matter, but it is sufficient that you have been shown or told about the incident.

The second rule is that the basis of your opinion must be of the type that "reasonably may be relied upon by experts in the field in forming an opinion on the matter in question." That is, the knowledge you draw upon and the methods you use must be the knowledge and methods that would be used by other experts in the same field in trying to solve the same problems. The basis of your opinion need not be admissible as evidence itself. For instance, you may use textbooks or articles as the basis for your opinion if they are generally acknowledged as authoritative sources on the subject. However, unusual or idiosyncratic use of information or methods may be challenged as an unacceptable basis for expert opinion.

The third rule is that you may not base your opinion on any matter which you are precluded by law from considering. For instance, you may not use an opinion testified to by another expert as a basis for your opinion. You may, however, use facts or the results of tests testified to by other experts as a basis for your opinion. You should exercise great caution with regard to matters which you are precluded from considering, because their mention in your testimony could result in a mistrial, with its attendant expense and loss of time. Before trial, you should consult with the attorney who has retained you about the admissibility of the basis that you intend to cite for your opinion.

The Direct Examination. Your testimony proper will begin with a direct examination by the attorney who has retained you. If the content and sequence of questions to be asked by the attorney have been adequately worked out in advance, the direct examination should hold no real surprises for you. A review of your plan for testimony before being called to the witness stand will help you to reply to the questions in a self-confident and authoritative manner. If the case has been a lengthy one, and if it is permitted, it may also be helpful to study the relevant portions of the transcript of court proceedings up to this point.

During direct examination, the sequence of questions regarding your expert opinion may follow several different patterns, but the questions will always cover certain basic areas. The attorney will ask you to explain what you were asked to do and how you went about gathering your information. You will be asked to describe any tests you performed and their results, and to describe any other investigations you carried out. You will be asked whether you have an opinion on a particular aspect of the subject in question. If you respond that you do, the attorney will then ask you to state your opinion. You should state your opinion without any elaboration. You will then be asked for the basis of your opinion. You may also be asked what possibilities you rejected or eliminated in forming your opinion. From this point on, you will explain how you arrived at your opinion, with or without further questions from the attorney.

The attorney's questions are limited by two major rules. First, a question must not "lead" the witness in what to say. Second, questions must not go outside the limits of the witness's expertise. Violation of either of these rules would probably result in the counsel for the opposition raising an immediate objection. Therefore, you will find that the most of the questions are short, that they are quite specific, and that they build on one another.

You must answer each question as it comes, and you should not attempt to anticipate later questions. To appear to volunteer information may make you seem eager to support your client's cause and detract from your position as a disinterested expert. The opposition attorney may object to statements which are not given in answer to a particular question. However, if a question is a complex one, give a complete answer, not just a "yes" or "no."

PROFESSIONAL PUBLICATIONS, INC.   Belmont, CA

You should also keep in mind that the attorney probably has a plan for the sequence of questions, and that it is not helpful to jump ahead to material that will be brought out later. You may assume that the attorney is trying to elicit evidence in the order that will be most effective. The procedures and restrictions of questioning may seem stultifying to you. Try to remember that they are part of a system which is designed to find the truth and render justice in disputes.

Your primary concern during this phase of testimony should be to communicate your opinion and its basis to the judge and jury. Assuming that you have a full grasp of your material, the main considerations are basically stylistic ones.

Since the most important members of your audience are the jurors, address them directly. It may seem more natural to face the attorney, since you are responding to his or her questions. In fact, it is best to face the attorney and listen attentively while a question is being asked. However, you will be more effective if you face the jury as you speak, directing your answers to them. Speak loudly and clearly enough that the judge and all jurors can hear you easily. Being aware of the importance of communicating to the jury, the attorney will probably take a position during questioning that will allow you to look both at him or her and at the jury while giving your answers.

Most of the points discussed in the section on the credibility of the deponent also apply to the credibility of the witness in court. Your style of dress, gestures, and speech will enhance your credibility if they are consistent with your expert role, and they will detract from it if they are not consistent with the role. An overly assertive, defiant, or arrogant manner is not only unattractive, but it may arouse suspicions about your competence. Let your qualifications speak for themselves. A modest but self-confident manner is the most effective.

Remember that few, if any, of the jurors will have any technical knowledge pertinent to the matter at issue in the trial—that is one of the reasons that you have been called upon to testify. This means that you cannot assume that they will understand technical terminology or jargon, or even that they will quickly comprehend the nature of the problem on which they must render a verdict. It is part of your job to educate the jury and give them an adequate understanding of your opinion.

Communication with the jury will be facilitated if you use straightforward, nontechnical language wherever you can, and if you explain the meaning of technical terms as simply as possible. Do not talk down to the jurors; they will resent it and you will lose credibility. At the same time, avoid inundating them with unfamiliar terms and overcomplicated explanations.

It is frequently helpful to show photographs, drawings, maps, charts, or models to illustrate the point you are discussing. If you make use of any visual aids, make sure that each juror is able to see them clearly.

In many cases, it is useful to produce such materials specifically for illustrative and educational purposes. The photographs, drawings, or models that you prepared during your investigation and which constitute part of the basis for your opinion may not be suitable or sufficient for demonstrating your point. During the pretrial period, you should discuss with the attorney whether visual aids will be useful during your testimony.

You will be allowed to refer to notes or other contents of your working file if necessary. If you request permission to consult your notes or other material, the court or opposing counsel may ask to inspect them.

At all times during your testimony, display complete impartiality, even though this may be difficult in the adversary atmosphere of a trial. Do not try to defend your client; stick to the facts which form the basis of your opinion. Do not exaggerate anything in your answers.

The attorney may overestimate the breadth of your competence. Do not let yourself get drawn into answering questions about subjects outside your specific field of expertise, even if you are generally knowledgeable about those subjects. If you do not know the answer to a question, simply say that you do not know. If you realize that you have made an error or left something out, correct yourself. Honesty and sincerity about your own limitations or mistakes are part of your ethical responsibility, and meeting that responsibility enhances your credibility.

The Cross-Examination. The cross-examination consists of questioning by counsel for the opposition on subjects that are within the scope of the direct examination. The cross-examination may encompass the areas of (1) your qualifications as an expert; (2) your opinion on the matter in question; (3) the basis for your opinion; and (4) any other matters covered in the direct examination. Cross-examination may not include questioning on the content or implications of any scientific or scholarly publication unless you have used the publication as part of the basis for your opinion, or unless it has been admitted in evidence by the court.

The purpose of cross-examination is to bring out evidence or aspects of the truth which were ignored or obscured in direct examination by testing the knowledge, recollection, and credibility of the witness. However, it is probably fair to say that the usual aim of the cross-examiner is to impeach (call into question) the credibility of the witness.

The cross-examination may be the most trying experience in the whole process of serving as an expert witness, and it will be the one which presents the greatest challenge to you as a person (not just as an expert). If the case has gone as far as trial testimony, the stakes are probably high, and attorneys for both sides will be under a great deal of pressure to win the case. They will be working hard to discredit the opposition, and the methods they use in cross-examination may cause a good deal of discomfort to the witnesses. If you are aware of some of the strategies and tactics that may be used, it may be easier for you to remain calm and avoid some of the traps that may be laid for you.

There are three main points of possible attack on credibility: qualifications, bias, and the testimony itself.

Cross-examination on qualifications takes place before opinion testimony begins, and it represents the opposition attorney's first chance to impeach your credibility. If you have given adequate consideration to the match between your qualifications and the nature of the case, you will probably not be disqualified by the judge. Nevertheless, there still may be some room for calling your qualifications into question.

For instance, the expert retained by the opposition may be more experienced than you, or the other expert may have written scholarly papers on the subject while you have not. The cross-examination may make much of your relative lack of experience in the hope of making the other expert seem more credible. Another possible strategy is to try to show that your expertise, while great in some areas, does not quite apply to the question at hand. Official designation as an expert, then, may not protect you from attacks on your qualifications, although it may substantially reduce their impact.

It is important not to act defensively under such attacks. If you can be provoked with derogatory inferences or a depreciatory tone, the opposition attorney will have made some progress in reducing your credibility.

PROFESSIONAL PUBLICATIONS, INC.   Belmont, CA

Answer questions on this subject, as on other subjects, factually, calmly, and in a self-confident manner.

If you have screened the case carefully for any possible conflict of interest, bias or interest should not be an actual problem. However, opposition counsel may raise the issue. You may be asked whether you are being compensated for your work on the case. If you are, you should say so. If asked the amount, you should state your fee and indicate that it is your normal fee for consulting. This should not constitute an issue, since the opposition expert is almost certainly receiving similar compensation, and the attorney for your client will be sure to bring this information out during cross-examination of that witness.

Potentially more serious would be attempts to show that you have any family, friendship, or business (including stock-holding) relations with your client or the client's attorney. Any of these relations could suggest that you are biased in favor of your client. This would imply that you cannot render an objective opinion, seriously undermining your credibility. Prudence dictates that you avoid all cases in which you have any such involvement, and that you avoid working too frequently with the same attorney. Frequent appearance as an expert witness for the same type of client (e.g., defendants in malpractice suits) may also suggest bias, and you should select your cases accordingly.

While you can forestall serious attacks on your credibility on the points of qualifications and bias by exercising good judgment in your selection of cases, there is little you can do to avoid an onslaught against your testimony regarding your expert opinion and its basis. Opposing counsel can be expected to put maximum effort into discrediting your opinion in any possible way.

The prime target for opposition counsel will be inconsistencies in your testimony. In order to find them, the opposition attorney will scrutinize your responses to interrogatories, your deposition, your written report, and possibly a review of your report by the opposition expert, who may have reached conclusions entirely different from yours. If you have previously testified in similar cases, your testimony in those cases may be reviewed. Any books or articles that you have written on the subject, or papers that you have delivered at professional conferences, may also be reviewed. Your earlier opinions and statements will be compared with your testimony under direct examination in the current trial.

One tactic is to ask a question similar to one asked in the deposition, but framed in a slightly different way, hoping to get you to give a different answer. A related tactic is to ask a series of questions to elicit your expert opinion and its basis in the current case, and then to quote a previous statement of yours which seems to contradict or be inconsistent with your present opinion. You may then be asked whether the quoted remarks were made by you, and you may be required simply to answer "yes" or "no," with no opportunity to explain the apparent inconsistency.

One aim of this tactic is to make you appear uncertain or confused about your opinions to the jury. Another aim is to frustrate and fluster you, reducing your effectiveness in your further testimony. Do not let yourself get upset by this tactic. If the quoted remarks are indeed yours, but you feel you can explain the inconsistency, simply say, "Yes, I can explain that." It is quite likely that you will not be given an adequate opportunity to explain during cross-examination, but you should be confident that the attorney who has called you as a witness will come back to the point in later redirect examination.

A second major target will be the assumptions on which you build your argument. If the opposition attorney (possibly relying on the advice of the opposition expert) can find a flaw in your reasoning, your credibility will be drastically lowered. The importance of thorough preparation, including consideration of all alternatives, cannot be overstressed.

Some attorneys will use various stylistic tactics to fluster you, trip you up, or otherwise reduce your credibility with the jury. For example, the cross-examiner may ask a particularly difficult question and then pressure you to answer immediately. You need not respond to the question with a rushed response. If further study, calculations, or the like are required for an adequate answer, say so. The court will instruct you in what to do in such an instance. Even if extra work is not required, you are entitled to enough time to think through your answer. On the other hand, when the answer to a question is immediately obvious, give it promptly.

The cross-examining attorney may ask a series of rapid-fire questions, or ask convoluted, multi-part questions in an attempt to elicit inconsistent answers or to confuse you, the judge, or the jury. You can deal with this type of questioning by being selective: "With regard to your first question, ..." Or you can ask the attorney to choose which question or part of a question you should answer. This technique will not only help to reduce your own errors or confusion, but it will also simplify the work of the jurors in their effort to understand the problem.

PROFESSIONAL PUBLICATIONS, INC.   Belmont, CA

Some questions are trick questions, designed to produce misleading answers. You may sometimes be compelled to respond to such questions with only a "yes" or "no." As in the case of apparent inconsistencies, you may follow your "yes" or "no" with an offer to explain. Or you may ask if the court will allow you to qualify your answer. Even if you are not allowed to explain, you will have called attention to the fact that the question may be misleading, and the attorney who has retained you will return to the subject during redirect examination.

Another tactic that may be used by some cross-examiners is to try to draw you into areas in which you are not fully expert. For instance, you may be asked to comment on books or other references which are not familiar to you. Or you may be asked to comment on problems which bear a superficial resemblance to the problem in question in the trial but which are actually outside your field of expertise. This tactic is designed to get you to voice a questionable opinion, and then to infer that all your opinions are questionable. Carefully delineate your area of expertise, and do not let yourself be drawn outside the boundaries. This is important in maintaining your credibility.

The authoritative status of various textbooks or articles may be one of the subjects of cross-examination, and you should be cautious in your remarks. You should not accept a particular source as authoritative unless you are thoroughly familiar with the sections that apply to the subject of your testimony. If you disagree with a source, do not hesitate to say so. Explain why you disagree, and indicate a source which you believe to be more correct.

Occasionally a cross-examiner will try to impeach your credibility by asking whether you have discussed the case with anyone. You should respond that you have discussed it extensively with the attorney who has called you as a witness. You may then be asked whether you have been told what to say. This may confuse you, since to some extent you will probably have rehearsed your testimony with the lawyer who has retained you. However, since it is your ethical responsibility to testify only to your honest opinions and the basis for them, and the attorney must respect that responsibility, your best response to such a question is that you have been instructed to tell the truth.

The cross-examiner may ask whether you have testified often as an expert witness. If you have, admit it freely. If asked for the details, give them. While the cross-examiner may be trying to imply that you are only an expert for hire, the fact that your opinion is frequently consulted is an indication of your professional competence and reputation.

PROFESSIONAL PUBLICATIONS, INC.   Belmont, CA

You may be asked whether your opinion is frequently different from that of other experts. If that is the case, you may say that "perhaps" or "sometimes" your opinion has been different from that of other experts, and that you believe you have been correct in those instances. Many problems are complex enough that experts may legitimately disagree.

During cross-examination, the attorney who has called you as witness may object to a question put by the cross-examiner. Listen carefully to the objection, as it may tell you what to beware of in the question. Then wait for the judge's decision as to whether or not you must answer the question.

You may be confronted with information that is detrimental to your client's case, or you may be asked a question, the correct answer to which will damage the client's case. In such a situation, simply acknowledge that the information is correct, or give the correct answer. Do not try to hedge or volunteer superfluous explanations. If you appear to be trying to hide something, you will lose credibility with the jury.

Never underestimate the cross-examining attorney. A competent attorney will, before trial, become thoroughly familiar with the subject in question. Any apparent ignorance is probably feigned, and may be designed to draw you into making a questionable statement which can then be discredited. In addition, he or she will know a good deal more than you about court procedures, examination techniques, and methods of persuading the jury. You should never try to outsmart an examining attorney; you will almost certainly be the loser. You will do best throughout testimony by maintaining a calm, fact-oriented attitude.

In a courtroom in which the attorney's physical location during questioning is not designated, the cross-examining attorney may take a position which makes it impossible to look at both the attorney and the jury at the same time. In such a situation, look at the attorney during a question, then turn to speak toward the jury while you are answering. Be alert to other maneuvers which may be designed to distract you from the jury. Do not look at the attorney who has engaged you; it may appear that you are expecting signs as to what you should say.

Some attorneys may shout, insult, and otherwise beleaguer an expert witness. It is important to remember that these are basically theatrical devices which are designed to induce you to behave in ways that will lower your credibility. Also remember that when the opposition attorney goes to great lengths to try to discredit you, it probably means that you are making a good impression on the jury. Therefore, you should try to maintain that high level of credibility. Shouting back is the worst thing you can do. A lawyer who shouts in court probably has a good deal of practice at public, theatrical shouting, whereas you probably have none. The lawyer will look effective, while you will look helplessly enraged. On the other hand, if you maintain a calm, courteous manner, the attorney's performance will appear aggressive and overblown, and you will win credibility points with the jury.

Throughout your testimony, but particularly during cross-examination, keep in mind these points for maintaining maximum credibility:

- Look the part of an expert. Dress appropriately, sit erect, and keep gestures to a minimum.

- Sound like an expert. Speak clearly and loudly enough for the jury to hear you easily.

- Talk like an expert. Be articulate but not verbose. Use "powerful" language.

- Communicate your ideas to the jury. Use clear, direct language and define technical terms.

- Listen carefully to the question being asked, and make sure you understand it before you answer. Ask for clarification if necessary.

- Answer only the question that is being asked.

- Tell the truth.

- Stay calm.

- Be polite.

If you follow these guidelines, prepare well before testimony, and cooperate with the attorney who has engaged you, you will have gone far toward ensuring that your appearance in court as expert witness will be successful.

The Redirect and Recross-Examinations. Following your cross-examination, the attorney who directly examined you may question you again on matters that came up during cross-examination. New subject matter or evidence cannot be brought up in redirect examination. The purpose of redirect examination is to clarify unclear or misleading points from the cross-examination. This part of testimony is also used to "rehabilitate" the impeached credibility of a witness.

The most common type of problem is an inconsistency between a statement given as part of a deposition and a statement given as part of court testimony. Frequently, the inconsistency can be attributed to the fact that you carried out further study or investigation after the time of the deposition, leading to some change in your testimony based on new knowledge. An explanation of this sort will usually restore any damage that was done to your credibility by the inconsistency.

A second common problem is that you will not have been able to answer a question fully or explain your answer to a question because of restrictions imposed by the cross-examining attorney. The redirect examination will give you an opportunity to clarify or explain the answers you gave during cross-examination. This may also be useful or necessary in the rehabilitation of your credibility.

Occasionally, the cross-examination will bring up an entirely new area of evidence or opinion. Redirect examination may cover the material of this new area.

The recross-examination is simply cross-examination over the points of contradiction between the cross-examination and the redirect examination. No new subjects may be brought up in recross-examination.

Ordinarily, you will not be examined any further after the recross-examination. However, it is within the judge's discretion to extend questioning under some circumstances. Also, the judge may ask questions of you either during or after your testimony.

After Testimony. At the close of your testimony, you will be excused from the witness stand. You will probably also be excused from the courtroom, and you should leave promptly. If you are not excused, you should follow the instructions of the attorney who has retained you. You will probably be asked to remain available for some specified period of time.

Even after you have finished testifying, you should continue to treat the case as confidential, and refrain from discussing it with others, particularly the opposition and its experts. You are obliged, as an expert witness, to keep all your files and materials, including exhibits used during testimony, until an official settlement of the case is reached. Since the verdict may be appealed or the case reopened through other legal means, you should retain these materials for at least a full year after formal notification that the case has been settled. If you have any questions about the disposal of these materials, you should discuss them with your client.

CLOSING OUT THE CASE   A case is closed in official terms as soon as a settlement is reached, whether in or out of court. The vast majority of cases you work on will be settled out of court. This may happen even while the trial is in progress. You may occasionally find that out-of-court settlement is reached after you give your testimony but before the jury retires. In a small minority of cases, the settlement will be determined by the court. Regardless of the method of settlement, the case is not yet closed for you, and you should budget a reasonable amount of time for closing the project out.

You should discuss with your client and the attorney the disposition of the materials which you have in your possession that are relevant to the case. After preserving all the relevant materials for a year after the settlement, you may destroy some of them by mutual consent. The client may ask you to return some documents, correspondence, and other materials, while you may wish to retain other items for your own files.

Where it seems possible and appropriate, discuss the trial with your client or the attorney. Try to get some feedback on the effectiveness of your testimony, including your organization of the evidence and your style of presentation. Ask their opinion about any exhibits (drawings, charts, graphs, models, etc.) that you developed and presented. This kind of feedback can help you to improve your performance as a witness in the future.

Your work ends when you render your final bill, and you may consider the case closed when you receive your final payment.

A NOTE ON ARBITRATION   Occasionally, a case you are asked to work on will be settled by arbitration rather than litigation. There are three types of cases for which arbitration may be sought: (1) cases in which the amount in question is below a certain level set by state statute, (2) cases in which both sides agree to arbitration rather than litigation in the hopes of a speedy and inexpensive resolution of the controversy, and (3) cases in which a contract with an arbitration clause is involved, generally a construction contract.

An expert witness is not usually called in the first two types of cases, as the expense may be greater than the utility of the service. It is more common for a consultant or expert to be called in arbitration-clause cases.

Although arbitration and litigation differ considerably, particularly in terms of formality and flexibility, the work of the consulting expert is much the same in both processes. There are only three main differences that may affect the expert's approach to the case.

The first main difference is that arbitration cases tend to be settled much more quickly than court cases. One reason is that discovery procedures are much more limited in arbitration cases. This means that depositions are not usually taken, although in some cases they may be. With limited pre-hearing discovery procedures, an arbitration case may proceed much more quickly than a litigation. Also, court trials must be fitted into a calendar in which criminal cases take precedence over civil cases, causing long delays. The fact that arbitration cases are not subject to such delays contributes to their speedy settlement.

The second main difference is the relative informality of the arbitration hearing, compared to the courtroom trial. In an arbitration hearing, witnesses are examined and cross-examined as they would be in a trial, but the rules of evidence and the procedures are more flexible. The pressure and the adversary atmosphere may be somewhat less in arbitration proceedings than in a trial.

Finally, perhaps the greatest difference from the point of view of the expert witness is that the "trier of fact" in a trial (a judge or jury) normally has no technical knowledge of the problem in question, while in arbitration proceedings the arbitrator may be an architect, engineer, or contractor who has some expertise in the subject area. This fact may reduce the expert witness's communication problems considerably.

On the whole, these differences will not affect your work if you are engaged for an arbitration case. The criteria for accepting a case, your contract and fees, your investigation, and your preparation for testimony will be essentially the same as in a litigated case.

ADMINISTRATION AND MANAGEMENT OF THE FORENSIC CASE Although information about administration of cases in which you do forensic work is scattered throughout this book, it may be useful to bring together some of the main points in one section.

Screening the Case. When you are first approached by a client, either directly or through an attorney, you should conduct a brief preliminary investigation to determine whether or not you wish to take the case. You should gather enough information to judge whether your expert qualifications fit the case, whether the client actually needs an expert, whether there are any ethical problems with the case, and whether you can work comfortably with the attorney. You should also prepare a preliminary estimate of the amount of work that you will need to do, and the fees that will be involved, and you should determine whether these are acceptable to the client. If the answers to these questions are positive, you may accept the case and enter an agreement with the client.

In entering an agreement, there are several matters that should be clarified and made explicit. You will need to know when to begin your work, exactly what work is expected of you, the extent of your responsibility and the responsibilities of others involved in the case, whether or not to submit a written report, the person you should report to, and how your work should be coordinated with that of any other experts. Perhaps the most basic matter is that of the contract and fees.

Fees. It will simplify your work in preparing fee estimates, as well as simplifying the work of the attorney in evaluating your estimate, if you have an established schedule of fees for various services. A sample of such a schedule follows:

Personnel (rate per hour)
- Principals
- Other engineers
- Draftsmen and technicians
- Clerical staff

PROFESSIONAL PUBLICATIONS, INC. Belmont, CA

Service categories
- Court appearance (full or half day)
- Field investigation (by hour or day)
- In-house investigation (by hour or day)
- Conferences (with attorney, client, etc.)
- Laboratory procedures (itemized)
- Travel to and from authorized destinations (by hour or day)

Miscellaneous services
- Services of sub-consultants
- Rental or construction of special equipment
- Construction of models or exhibits
- Use of test equipment (in-house)
- Storage of evidence
- Reproductions and photocopies

Miscellaneous charges
- Transportation (airfare, etc.)
- Mileage
- Parking
- Lodging and meals
- Telephone
- Other

Many consultants have an hourly or per diem fee which they apply to all of their work, including forensic cases. Some of them indicate a range of fees for various services, depending on whether the work involved is routine or extraordinary, and they bill service categories and miscellaneous charges at cost plus a percentage to cover administrative expenses. Others charge the same hourly or daily fee regardless of the type of service. Many consultants charge time-and-a-half for work on Sundays and holidays or for work in excess of eight hours in one day.

Because it is so difficult to estimate the amount of time and work that a case will involve, few consultants charge on a lump-sum or fixed-fee basis. You should choose the fee basis which suits you and your circumstances best.

Most forensic engineers require the advance payment of a retainer fee before beginning work on a case. They then charge their fees against the retainer until it is used up, at which time they commence billing on a monthly or other regular basis.

A retainer fee may be particularly advisable where the client may not be able to afford the full range of services that the case requires, or where the expected settlement is not great enough to justify the full expense of an expert consultant. With such clients it is especially important to be clear on the extent of investigation which you believe will be necessary and on the anticipated cost to the client. If the client appears indecisive, it may be advisable to set a minimum fee for preliminary consultation, with further services and fees to be negotiated at a later point.

It is best to come to an explicit understanding at the beginning as to the amount of the retainer (if you require one), the frequency of billing, and the person to whom you should submit your bills. If you have definite requirements on these issues, you should make them clear to the client. You should also learn at the beginning who will be responsible for paying your fees. You should insist on prompt payment. If there is any tendency toward late payment, make it clear that your continuing work on the case is contingent upon businesslike payment of bills.

When your client is an insurance company acting on behalf of a defendant, the payment system may be complicated by a deductible policy. In this situation, you may be required to bill the defendant, not your client, up to the deductible amount. This type of complication can result in delays in payment up to several months, and you should be prepared to wait for a long time to collect your fees. If such delays are unacceptable, you may prefer not to accept the case.

Most clients will wish to have a statement of services which have been rendered during the billing period. Some will require considerable detail, including a daily breakdown of services and their unit cost. Others may be content with somewhat less detail. Whatever the degree of detail, the monthly or other interim statement is useful to the client in maintaining records of the costs of litigation. Before beginning your billing, you should learn what the client requires in the way of a statement of services.

It is always best to be paid up to date before testifying in court. You may be asked during cross-examination whether your client owes you any money, in the hope of suggesting that your testimony may be influenced by monetary considerations. If you are paid up to date, it will be difficult to create an issue and attack your credibility on this point.

The Contract. The document which summarizes all these agreements regarding the amount of your work, your fees, and the client's payment schedule is the contract. The attorney who has retained you may draw up a contract. You should read it carefully before signing to be certain that it includes all the conditions you wish it to have and that it does not contain anything that you would object to. Be sure that it includes a specific statement to the effect that payment to you is in no way contingent on the results of your work or on the outcome of the litigation.

You may prefer to use a standard contract with all clients, in which case you may wish to consult an attorney on the form which would best suit your circumstances. You may also prefer to allow a third party, such as a referral service, to draw up and administer the contract.

Whatever the type or source of your contract, you should insist on signing a contract or at least obtaining a written confirmation of the engagement of your services before beginning work on a case. Even your preliminary investigation will take a good deal of your time, and it may constitute a valuable service for the client. Therefore, you should have a written agreement and begin charging for your services from the very beginning of the case.

Fees Charged to Opposing Counsel. As a general rule, all of your services will be charged to your client. The exception is the deposition you give to opposing counsel. Although in some cases your client will be responsible for your deposition fee, usually the attorney who requests the deposition is responsible for compensating you. You may charge for the time you spend giving the deposition and the time you spend traveling to and from the site of the deposition. The fee you charge must be your normal fee (hourly, half-day, or daily). If the reasonableness of your fee is challenged, the court may rule on the amount you are allowed to charge. The time spent in preparation for a deposition is charged to your client, not to the opposition.

You may simply submit a statement for your time to the attorney who requested the deposition. Alternatively, you may submit an estimate based on the anticipated length of the deposition and require payment in advance. If the deposition takes more time than originally estimated, you may bill later for the difference between the advance payment and the total fee. The attorney who has retained you can advise you on the procedure for advance billing for depositions.

FORENSIC ENGINEERING AS A BUSINESS   Engineers who testify as expert witnesses generally fall into one of three categories: (1) those who testify only once or twice, under special circumstances; (2) those who work as expert witnesses occasionally, as part of a larger consulting practice; and (3) those who devote most or all of their professional effort to forensic engineering. Engineers in the first group tend not to look upon expert witnessing as part of their business, and those in the third group usually work with firms or other organizations which manage their contacts, referrals, case assignments, contracts, and other administrative matters. It is the second group to which this section is especially addressed.

Establishing a Reputation as an Expert. If you are an individual consulting engineer seeking to add forensic engineering to your practice, your first priority should be to establish a reputation as an expert in your field. This requires not only a good educational background but demonstrated competence as well. In some areas of engineering, product development experience is particularly important. If you have administrative or business experience, in addition to your technical experience, your value as an expert consultant or witness may be greatly increased.

Another important credential for an expert witness is active membership and participation in professional societies and groups. It is helpful if you have authored professional books or articles and have given technical papers at meetings of professional societies. Patented inventions or professional awards are also valuable additions to your qualifications.

You should maintain an updated resume which lists your education, experience, and professional accomplishments. Reprints or annotated bibliographies of your published work should be appended to the resume. This will be helpful to prospective clients in evaluating your suitability for their cases.

The most effective and sought-after experts have a number of other qualities and qualifications in addition to their expertise in a particular field. Although you may be an expert only in a relatively narrow area, it is to your advantage to have a broad knowledge of the field surrounding your specialty. You should also be willing to devote time and effort to studying a problem and to reviewing related subjects.

It is helpful to be familiar with legal procedure and legal and insurance terminology. Depending on your field of expertise, you will need to be familiar with relevant statutes and ordinances. This is particularly applicable to all areas involved in construction, but is true for many other specialties as well. You should learn something about such concepts as entitlement, breach of warranty, and sound value, as well as negligence, strict liability, foreseeability, connection, and intervening causes. You will be called upon to make judgments about the probability of harm and the gravity of a risk in evaluating negligence, and you should learn how legal professionals define these terms. A good working knowledge of the rules of evidence will make you a more effective and useful witness.

A firm understanding of cost and value is an important asset for the expert witness. Most if not all of the litigation cases you work with will hinge on the question of financial cost and equitable compensation, and you may often be called upon for estimates of fair cost. Certification by the American Association of Cost Engineers would augment your reputation.

A forensic engineer may spend less than three per cent of his or her time actually testifying in court. Nevertheless, personality may play a crucial role in your reputation as an expert witness. Sometimes a great expert proves to be a poor witness because of personality traits that negatively influence performance on the witness stand. Those who are experienced in forensic engineering describe the ideal witness as a person who has "no ego problems."

This description encompasses a number of traits. You may wish to compare your own typical behavior with these traits. For example, you should be relatively free of the sorts of fears, such as fear of public speaking, which would have a negative influence on performance. You should not be overly sensitive to criticism. As an expert witness, you will be subject to a great deal of direct and implied criticism, some of it from your professional colleagues who testify for the opposition. You should not be quick-tempered or argumentative. Rather, you should be able to stay calm despite the provocations of the cross-examiner.

In addition to the absence of negative traits, the presence of positive traits is desirable. For instance, you should be articulate, and you should be able to think clearly under the pressure of cross-examination. You should be able to communicate your ideas in an easily comprehensible manner. You should be able to remain objective despite the adversary atmosphere of the courtroom. You should also be loyal and discreet.

Some of these qualities are as much a product of experience as of character. Your first experience of cross-examination will probably seem quite challenging, even if you do not ordinarily suffer from anxiety, inarticulateness, or bad temper. A disappointing first performance need not discourage you from the practice of forensic engineering. However, you should try to assess your performance honestly. If you believe that you can learn from your mistakes and improve your performance in the future, by all means try to do so. On the other hand, if you find the experience distressing rather than challenging, you may decide that continuing with forensic engineering would be the wrong choice for you. If you decide to continue with this type of work, you can expect further practice to lead to greater ease and confidence in your performance.

If you can combine genuine expertise with effective courtroom performance, you will be well on your way to establishing your reputation as an excellent expert witness.

Finding Referrals. In the long run, your best form of advertising is word of mouth. Attorneys and other clients who have been satisfied with your work will refer you to their colleagues who are seeking an expert consultant. Your own engineering colleagues who are familiar with your work will refer potential clients to you. In the short run, however, you may need a more systematic approach to marketing.

There are a variety of associations, firms, and agencies which specialize in providing the names of experts to clients who are seeking consultation in legal cases.

The association which appears to apply the most stringent criteria for membership and listing is the National Academy of Forensic Engineers (NAFE), based in Alexandria, Virginia. NAFE is affiliated with the National Society of Professional Engineers (NSPE), and has as its purpose the identification of valid practitioners of forensic engineering, and the promotion of their continuing education in the field. Acceptance for membership in NAFE depends on a number of criteria: each member must be a professional engineer, a member of NSPE, and a member of a technical engineering society in "an acceptable grade." Other considerations are a record of considerable experience in forensic engineering, including actual court testimony, and recommendations by attorneys or senior claims managers in the insurance industry. NAFE membership, then, appears to be reserved for forensic engineers with relatively extensive courtroom experience and professional prominence. When your qualifications meet NAFE requirements, membership will certainly be beneficial to your career.

Many attorneys who are routinely engaged in product-liability litigation keep lists of experts in various fields of engineering. Potential sources for names on the lists include nearby universities or testing laboratories and the recommendations of colleagues. When an attorney is pleased with the performance of an expert (including an expert engaged by the opposition), his or her name will be added to the list. The list may then be used throughout the attorney's firm, or shared with colleagues who are seeking expert witnesses. Having your name on a lawyer's list of experts can be a good source of referrals, but it is a limited source.

You may be listed in the yellow pages of the telephone directory, conforming to the advertising standards of your professional society. However, many forensic engineers find that yellow pages listing is a rather indiscriminate approach, which may lead to loss of time in screening callers who are not seeking the particular professional services that you offer.

The professional societies to which you belong may be valuable sources of referrals. This is particularly likely to be true if you are active and visible in the society, so that other members are aware of you and your accomplishments. Some societies publish directories of members in which you may list your services.

If you meet the criteria for being listed, listing in *Engineers of Distinction: A Who's Who in Engineering* may be useful.

The American Bar Association maintains a Register of Expert Witnesses. You may be included in the register by submitting a resume which outlines your education and experience and gives the names of references who are familiar with your work as an expert consultant.

There are two other organizations which maintain lists of expert witnesses. One of these is the Defense Research Institute (DRI), a Chicago-based organization of attorneys, which has established an Expert Witness Index. The other listing service is maintained by the National Forensic Center, which publishes a Forensic Services Directory, and also supplies lists of all types of experts to Westlaw's Computer-based Forensic Services Directory.

You may register for the DRI Index by sending a resume. Since the index is classified by area of expertise, you should specify in detail the areas in which you believe you are an expert. The references you name should include attorneys or insurance companies who have engaged you as an expert consultant or witness. You should also list the names of cases in which you have been involved (e.g., Smith vs. Jones, 1983, with the name and location of the court in which the case was heard). You may be listed in the index even though you have no previous courtroom experience.

Listing in the Forensic Services Directory is similarly accomplished by sending a detailed resume, including your areas of expertise and previous forensic experience, to the National Forensic Center.

Both the DRI Index and the Westlaw Computer-based Directory act as simple referral services for their members. When an expert in a given field is being sought, these services will provide names and resumes of appropriate listees, as close as possible to the geographical area of the inquirer. The attorney or firm seeking the expert is then responsible for making the contacts and evaluating the qualifications of the experts whose names have been provided. The experts contacted are likewise responsible for screening the proposed case.

There are other organizations, usually operating at a local level, which try to match attorneys or other prospective clients with appropriate expert consultants. These are known variously as expert-witness employment agencies, clearing houses, and brokerage houses.

Their usual mode of operation is to advertise their services, to act as the point of contact between the expert and the client, to administer the contract, billing, and other details, and to finance their operations by charging the client a percentage of the expert's fee. The expert receives his or her customary fee from the broker. This type of service may not be the first choice of clients, because it usually means increased expense. On the other hand, it may be the most efficient way to find a local expert with specific qualifications, which may offset the disadvantage of the extra expense. The expert may also find the arrangement advantageous, as the broker finds referrals and manages administrative details at no cost to the expert.

If you do some of your work through a broker of this sort, it is advisable to follow the usual procedures in evaluating each case. You cannot depend on the broker to refer to you only cases which you will find acceptable. You must evaluate each case independently, declining to undertake those which are inappropriate. This is necessary to maintain your professional reputation.

How Much of Your Practice Should Be Devoted to Forensic Engineering? As you begin to build up a larger referral base, you may find that you are spending more and more of your time on forensic cases. At that point you may wish to consider some of the pros and cons of moving into a largely forensic practice.

There seem to be two main issues: maintenance of expert status and maintenance of credibility.

When you are spending a good deal of your time learning about the jurisprudence system and assessing matters such as cost and responsibility, you may have less time available for following the literature in your field or for taking on design or product development projects. Consequently, you may feel that you are losing your expertise. On the other hand, the research you are doing to support your opinions in each case may be adding to your expertise. Also, you may feel that your growing familiarity with the jurisprudence system constitutes a new field of expertise, and that you are developing a broader professional base.

This is a balance that you must evaluate for yourself, because the situation may be different for each individual. The one certainty is that true expertise is the prime requisite for forensic engineering. If you wish to continue your work as an expert witness, you must allocate your time and effort in such a way as to maintain and extend your expert knowledge.

The credibility issue revolves around the question of exposure, or the frequency with which one testifies as an expert witness. There appear to be two schools of thought on this question.

The first argues that too much exposure is bad for your reputation and credibility. It is an unfortunate fact that some engineers, acting quite unprofessionally, have made a practice of rendering favorable "expert" opinions for well-paying clients. Naturally, these individuals have quickly acquired an unfavorable reputation among legal professionals. If you appear frequently in court as an expert witness, you run the risk of opposition counsel attempting to pin the same reputation on you.

The fact that many attorneys are wary of experts who have testified many times may be to your benefit while you are getting started in forensic engineering.

The second school of thought argues that frequent invitations to testify as an expert witness are a confirmation of your expert status and can only enhance your reputation. There are many forensic engineers whose entire professional activity consists of forensic work and who manage to maintain high credibility, because they are truly experts and they adhere to the highest professional and ethical standards.

If you choose your cases carefully, maintain your expert status, and testify truthfully in all cases, it is unlikely that frequent appearance as an expert witness will have an adverse effect on your reputation.

Management Issues in Forensic Engineering. One of the hallmarks of forensic engineering is that it calls for the work of more than one person. In the simplest case, you must coordinate your work with that of the attorney who has engaged you. In more complex cases, you may also have to coordinate your work with that of other experts working on the case. You may have to direct the work of laboratory technicians or other assistants. Whenever coordination of effort is required, management becomes an issue.

Early in a case, you will want to clarify the division of labor. You should assume that the attorney who has engaged you is the leader of the team, and that it is the attorney who will make the final decisions as to the extent of your investigation, the use of exhibits during testimony, and other similar questions that might arise.

If you disagree with these decisions, you should discuss them with the attorney. For instance, if the limitations being put on your investigation will, in your view, make it impossible for you to form a valid opinion, you should point this out. However, as the architect of the legal strategy to be used in the case, the attorney must have the final right of decision. If you cannot reach agreement on fundamental issues, it may be best to withdraw from the case.

It is best to get a clear statement of exactly what is expected of you, and you should make it clear exactly what you can contribute. You cannot be required to win the case for the client, nor can you be required to find evidence that will be favorable to the client. Neither can you be expected to be infallible. However, you can rightfully be expected to work with the thoroughness, care, and competence which would justify your status as expert. You can and should commit yourself to carrying out a thorough investigation, to reporting all the facts, and to providing an expert opinion.

You can also be expected to be loyal to your client and to the attorney, at least to the point of not discussing the case with outsiders, staying with a case until its conclusion, and doing what you can to minimize cost to the client. This loyalty does not imply that you will favor your client's position, if not supported by the facts. Keep in mind that it does more harm than good to tell the client what he or she wants to hear. Opposition counsel, and opposition experts, will make short work of an inadequate claim.

After you have reached agreement on precisely what your responsibilities will be, you should set up a schedule for communication with the attorney. Since the attorney's strategy may depend heavily on your findings, you should keep him or her informed of the progress of your work on a regular basis. The attorney should also keep you informed of major developments, such as the engagement of other experts or the discovery of new evidence relevant to your investigation.

If other experts are working on the case, it is usually helpful to coordinate your work with theirs, conferring jointly with the attorney. In some cases, the work of experts may involve a certain amount of conflict. For example, each of you may need to conduct tests on the same part or material, and the use of one test may make the other tests impossible to conduct. Such problems should be solved in conference with the attorney. Because of these potential conflicts, it is essential that each of you be kept informed of the other's planned activities.

In some cases it will be impossible for you personally to conduct all of the laboratory work that you consider necessary. In these cases, you will probably delegate that portion of the work to a testing laboratory, or to a technician in your own firm. When it is necessary for you to delegate some of your work in this fashion, you should be careful to give explicit instructions for what is to be done. Where possible, you should also observe the testing; if you have not actually seen the outcome of the test, the technician may have to be called to testify.

In all of the relationships that you may be involved in while working on a forensic case—whether with your client, the attorney, other experts, technicians, or assistants in your own firm—the key to success is clear and explicit communication. If both you and the other person know precisely what each expects of the other, each of you can proceed with your own work, confident that you will not encounter unpleasant surprises when it is too late to do anything about them.

PROFESSIONAL PUBLICATIONS, INC.   Belmont, CA

ETHICAL   As a forensic engineer, you have a complex set
CONSIDERATIONS   of ethical responsibilities.

As a licensed professional, you have a social trust. In granting you a license, the state gives you certain rights and privileges. In return, it sets certain standards for the conduct of your business. Your adherence to those standards is not only legally required, but it is a responsibility that you owe to the public.

As a member of a professional community, you have the responsibility of representing that community every time you render professional services. This means that you must conduct your business on a strictly professional level.

In every aspect of your business, from generating referrals to giving testimony in court, your conduct must conform to the standards set by members of your profession. Your advertising should conform to the recommendations of your professional society. You may refer clients to a colleague, or vice-versa, but fee-splitting in such cases is unethical. You must strictly avoid cases in which conflict of interest may be an issue. You may not make your compensation contingent on the outcome of any case.

As a party to a contract with your client, you have responsibilities to the client. You owe the client a thorough investigation, and an honest, carefully considered opinion. You also owe the client confidentiality; the case should not be discussed with anyone except the attorney and other persons that he or she authorizes. You should not withdraw from a case without good cause. You should be willing to integrate your work with the overall legal strategy planned by the attorney. You should be willing to learn the skills that will make you an effective witness.

Finally, as a citizen testifying under oath, you have the responsibility to tell the truth: to report the facts as you know them, and to give your honest opinion.

Honesty is the cornerstone of your ethical responsibilities. As one author put it, "the product is on trial only once, but the technical expert's professional reputation is on trial every time he forms and defends an opinion." Honest testimony and honest business conduct will form a solid foundation for your professional reputation and success.

COULD YOU BE A FORENSIC ENGINEER? If you believe that you qualify as an expert, and you are interested in trying your hand as an expert witness, you have a good chance for success. Consumer protection legislation, court doctrines of strict liability, and a general move toward litigation as a means of settling disputes have greatly increased the number of product liability cases. Experts in all engineering specialties are being sought for consultation and testimony in these cases. In short, the market for expert witnesses is growing.

The rewards of forensic engineering can be very satisfying, if you are suited to the work. The financial rewards are at least as great as in any other branch of consulting engineering, and sometimes much greater. The challenges may be considerable. The technical problems are often complex and demanding, a test of your professional capabilities. The rigors of testifying may challenge you both professionally and personally. The role of forensic engineer will require you to enlarge your perspective, to look at a problem from the points of view of all parties involved, to work toward a resolution of issues, and yet to form an objective opinion and support it effectively. Meeting these challenges successfully may be one of the most satisfying rewards of your career.

PROFESSIONAL PUBLICATIONS, INC.   Belmont, CA

SUGGESTED READING

If this book has whetted your interest in forensic engineering, it will have served its purpose. Now you may wish to begin to take concrete steps toward giving it a try.

If you are not yet a registered professional engineer, registration should be your first step. Several of the books published by Professional Publications, Inc. can be of assistance to you in taking this step.

First, it is recommended that you read *How to Become a Professional Engineer*. This book will guide you through each phase of the examination and registration process.

Next, if you are at the beginning of the registration process, you will find the *Engineer-in-Training Reference Manual* very helpful in preparing for the first-level (Engineer-in-Training, or EIT) examination. Quick reference summary cards and examples of examinations, with solutions, are also available.

If you are preparing for the second-level or Professional Engineer examination, you will find review manuals for civil engineering, mechanical engineering, electrical engineering, and chemical engineering. In addition, there are books on special topics, such as seismic design and timber design for civil engineers.

Useful to anyone taking the examinations, but of special interest to anyone who is interested in becoming an expert witness, is *Engineering Law, Ethics, and Liability*.

For detailed information on any of these books, write to Professional Publications, Inc., 1250 Fifth Avenue, Belmont, CA 94002, or call (415) 593-9119 to request a catalog of publications.

BIBLIOGRAPHY

Aronson, Robert B. "The expert witness: Why he is needed." *Machine Design*, July 7, 1977, pp. 64-67.

Brown, Seymour W. "Types of clients and services." *Consulting Engineer*, January 1984, pp. 53-55.

Consulting Engineers Association of California, *The Consulting Engineer As Expert Witness*, 2nd Ed. CEAC, 1983.

Hough, James E. "The engineer as expert witness." *Civil Engineering*, December 1981, pp. 56-58.

Jacobson, Richard A. "The prestige way to moonlight: Be an expert witness." *Machine Design*, November 15, 1973, pp. 132-136.

Manzi, Joseph E. "The expert witness." *Consulting Engineer*, October 1984, pp. 80-84.

McQuillan, Joseph A. "The CE as expert witness." *Consulting Engineer*, January 1984, pp. 48-50.

Pritzker, Paul E. "Investigative Techniques." *Consulting Engineer*, January 1984, pp. 44-47.

Pritzker, Paul E. "The primary aspects of forensic engineering." *Consulting Engineer*, October 1978, pp. 22-26.

Specter, Marvin M. "Engineering applied to jurisprudence." *Consulting Engineer*, January 1984, pp. 42-43.

Szews, A.P. "The engineer as technical expert." *Machine Design*, July 26, 1979, pp. 106-109.

Talbot, Thomas F. "Your day in court." *Machine Design*, February 6, 1975, pp. 68-72.

APPENDIX A

SAMPLE CONTRACT: INDIVIDUAL CONSULTANT OR SMALL FIRM

FEES AND CONDITIONS

This agreement is entered into on the date of _____ between _____, hereinafter to be known as Expert, and _____, hereinafter to be known as Client.

Billing rates:

Retainer fee: _____, payable in advance, unused portion returned, applied to final invoice only.

Terms: Net 30 days. A _____% monthly finance charge (_____% annual percentage rate) will be added to all past due accounts.

Time spent in travel related to the assignment will be charged at hourly rates, except that no more than eight (8) hours of travel time will be charged in any day.

Overnight accommodations and air travel will be billed at cost.

Miscellaneous materials and expenses (copies, photographs, telephone, etc., will be billed at cost plus _____% service charge.

Automobile mileage rate: $_____ per mile.

Client agrees to pay all collection expenses, related attorney's fees, and any legal costs incurred in collection. Client further agrees that compensation for Expert's services are not contingent upon the payment to, or performance of, any other parties, nor is compensation contingent upon the results of Expert's investigation.

Expert warrants that services are performed with the limits prescribed by Client with the usual thoroughness and competence of the profession. No other warranty or representation, either expressed or implied, is included in Expert's proposals, contracts, or work products.

In retaining Expert, Client agrees to the above fees and terms.

Client	Client	
Name_____	Firm_____	Date_____
_____	_____	_____
_____	_____	_____

Source: Volk & Associates, Inc., Oakland, California, an expert witness clearing house. (Adapted from the original.)

PROFESSIONAL PUBLICATIONS, INC.   Belmont, CA

APPENDIX B

SAMPLE CONTRACT: LARGE ENGINEERING FIRM

TERMS AND CONDITIONS OF AGREEMENT

CHARGES

Work performed on a time-and-expense basis will be charged in accordance with Consultant Firm's current "Schedule of Rates and Charges," attached.

Any unusual types of work not specifically covered by the "Schedule of Rates and Charges" are charged at a rate determined to be reasonable in relation to the type of work performed.

Work performed under fixed price contracts will be charged at the agreed fixed amount.

TERMS OF PAYMENT

Periodic statements are rendered, usually monthly, and are due immediately upon receipt. Outstanding balances past due over thirty days are subject to a delinquency charge of one and one-half per cent per month until paid. Consultant Firm, without liability, may withhold delivery of reports and other data and may suspend performance of its obligations to Client pending full payment of all charges.

EXECUTION OF SCOPE OF SERVICES

Consultant Firm will perform all work in accordance with generally accepted professional engineering practice. No other warranty, express or implied, is made concerning work performed under the agreement, including findings, recommendations, specifications, or professional advice.

Consultant Firm will diligently proceed with the work contracted for and will provide its report in a timely manner, except for delays occasioned by factors beyond its control, or by factors which were not reasonably foreseeable, or initiated by Client.

Work under the agreement will be terminated upon receipt by Consultant Firm of written notice from Client, provided that Consultant Firm may complete such analyses, records, and reports as are reasonably necessary to protect its professional reputation and adequately document the work performed through termination. In such event, a termination charge not exceeding ten per cent of all charges incurred through termination may be made at the discretion of Consultant Firm.

MISCELLANEOUS

Client agrees that the aggregate liability of Consultant Firm to Client and any other persons or entities arising from performance of this agreement, including costs of defense and attorney fees, shall be limited to a sum not exceeding the lesser of $_____ or the contract value on account of any and all injury or damage to person or property, any design defect, error, omission, or professional negligence. Client hereby releases and agrees to indemnify and hold Consultant Firm and its employees and consultants free and harmless from any such liability to Client or any third parties to the extent the aggregate of such liability exceeds the lesser of $_____ or the contract amount.

Consultant Firm will hold in strictest confidence all proprietary information and trade secrets of the Client to which it may be given access. Unless otherwise expressly agreed in writing, all reports, recommendations, procedures and other information provided to the Client under this agreement shall be the joint property of the Client and Consultant Firm, and may be used without restriction by either. However, unless otherwise expressly agreed in writing, Consultant Firm shall retain exclusive rights to all proprietary information, technologies, trade secrets, inventions, or patentable ideas developed during performance of this agreement.

In the event a lawsuit between Client and Consultant Firm arises under this agreement, such lawsuit shall be filed and tried only in a court of competent jurisdiction within _____County, _____, and the prevailing party in any action shall recover from the losing party his reasonable attorney fees and costs of suit incurred, in addition to any other relief granted.

SCHEDULE OF RATES AND CHARGES

PROFESSIONAL FEES

Principal Engineer	$_____ - $_____ /hour
Managing Engineer	$_____ - $_____ /hour
Staff Consultant	$_____ - $_____ /hour
Senior Engineer	$_____ - $_____ /hour
Engineer	$_____ - $_____ /hour
Research Specialist	$_____ - $_____ /hour
Technical Assistant/ Engineering Technician	$_____ - $_____ /hour
Administrative/Nontechnical Assistant	$_____ - $_____ /hour

The above hourly rates represent the Professional Fees charged by Consultant Firm for work performed within the continental United States. A rate is established for each employee within his/her functional classification, based on a person's individual qualifications and experience. These rates are modified periodically at the discretion of Consultant Firm. For projects conducted outside the continental United States, premium rates may be applied to adjust for cost of living differentials. Payment is required in U.S. dollars within thirty (30) days after receipt of invoice, or penalties may be applied.

SPECIAL PRODUCTS

Specialized software, methodologies, or other technical products developed by Consultant Firm will be charged at rates which reflect development costs and equivalent technical value. Specific prices and conditions will be provided upon request.

EQUIPMENT CHARGES

Equipment Name _____ $_____ / hour

Testing or data processing equipment may be charged at rates not to exceed equivalent rental rates from commercial leasing companies or comparable data processing service companies.

OTHER PROJECT EXPENSES

Travel and personal expenses are charged at cost. Air travel is charged at the most effective fare basis for the project involved. Local mileage is charged at _____ cents per mile.

Special project expenses requiring nonroutine administrative processing are charged at cost plus fifteen per cent (15%). These include materials, equipment, outside laboratory tests, outside computer charges, special printing and reproduction, shipping charges, special fees, extra insurance, etc.

Source: Failure Analysis Associates, Inc., Menlo Park, California, a forensic engineering firm. (Adapted from the original.)

APPENDIX C

ADDRESSES OF PROFESSIONAL AGENCIES AND ASSOCIATIONS

1. American Association of Cost Engineers (AACE)
   P.O. Box 1557
   Morgantown, West Virginia 26507-1557
   Telephone: (304) 296-8444

2. American Bar Association (ABA)
   750 N. Lakeshore Drive
   Chicago, Illinois 60611
   Telephone: (312) 988-5000

3. American Society of Trial Consultants
   Department of Speech and Mass Communication
   Towson State University
   Towson, Maryland 21204
   Telephone: (301) 830-2448

4. Defense Research and Trial Lawyers Association (DRI)
   Expert Witness Index
   750 North Lakeshore Drive, Suite 500
   Chicago, Illinois 60611
   Telephone: (312) 944-0575

5. National Academy of Forensic Engineers (NAFE)
   Contact through:
   NSPE
   1420 King Street
   Alexandria, Virginia 22314
   Telephone: (703) 684-2800

6. National Forensic Center
   17 Temple Terrace
   Lawrenceville, New Jersey 08648
   Telephone: (609) 883-0550

7. National Society for Professional Engineers (NSPE)
   1420 King Street
   Alexandria, Virginia 22314
   Telephone: (703) 684-2800

APPENDIX D

CONDUCTING A LITERATURE SEARCH

An important part of a forensic engineer's investigation of a case is the determination of applicable legal and industry standards. Standards are generally published by federal agencies, professional organizations, and manufacturers. The following are suggested as sources of information that may be useful to many forensic engineers.

AGENCIES

Occupational Safety and Health Administration (OSHA)
OSHA is a federal agency within the U.S. Department of Labor. It is the source for legal codes, regulations, and acts governing standards. OSHA may be contacted through regional offices of the U.S. Department of Labor.

American National Standards Institute (ANSI)
11 West 42nd Street
New York, New York 10036
Telephone: (212) 642-4900

American Society for Testing and Materials (ASTM)
1916 Race Street
Philadelphia, Pennsylvania 19103-1187
Telephone: (215) 977-9679

Canadian Standards Association (CSA)
178 Rexdale Boulevard
Rexdale (Toronto)
Ontario M9W 1R3
Canada
Telephone: (416) 747-4000

International Standards Organization (ISO)
Contact through ANSI.

National Fire Protection Association
    Batterymarch Park
    Quincy, Massachusetts 02269-9101
    Telephone: (617) 770-3000

    This agency publishes a number of codes, including the National
    Electrical Code.

National Safety Council (NSC)
    444 N. Michigan Avenue
    Chicago, Illinois 60611
    Telephone: (312) 527-4806

    NSC publishes the NSC Data Sheets, a series of papers dealing with
    safety considerations for specific products and activities, along with
    other standards.

Society of Automotive Engineers (SAE International)
    400 Commonwealth Drive
    Warrendale, Pennsylvania 15096-0001
    Telephone: (412) 776-4841

Underwriters Laboratories (UL)
    Publications Stock
    333 Pfingsten Road
    Northbrook, Illinois 60062
    Telephone: (708) 272-8800

DIRECTORIES AND INDICES

Directory of Corporate Affiliations
    National Register Publishing Company
    121 Chanlon Road
    New Providence, New Jersey 07974
    Telephone: (800) 521-8110

    This directory is an excellent source when checking for conflicts of
    interest.

The Directory of Directories
   Gale Research Company
   835 Penobscot Building
   Detroit, Michigan 48226-4094
   Telephone: (313) 961-2242

The Encyclopedia of Associations
   Gale Research Company
   835 Penobscot Building
   Detroit, Michigan 48226-4094
   Telephone: (313) 961-2242

Index and Directory of U.S. Industry Standards
   Information Handling Services
   15 Inverness Way East
   Englewood, Colorado 80150
   Telephone: (303) 790-0600

Index of Federal Specifications, Standards, and
Commercial Item Descriptions (FPMR 101-29.1)
   General Services Administration
   Federal Supply Service Bureau—Specifications Section
   470 East L'Enfant Plaza SW, Suite 8100
   Washington, D.C. 20407
   Telephone: (202) 755-0325

An Index of U.S. Voluntary Engineering Standards
   Publication & Program Information
   National Institute of Standards & Technology
   Gaithersburg, MD 20899
   Telephone: (301) 975-2000

National Trade and Professional Associations of the U.S.
   Columbia Books, Inc.
   1212 New York Avenue NW
   Suite 330
   Washington, D.C. 20005
   Telephone: (202) 898-0662

INDEX

advertising, 58
after testimony, 48
agreement, 51
ambiguities, 19
American Bar Association, 58
arbitration, 49, 50
attorney-client privilege, 25, 26

basis for opinion, 41
behavior, 31
bias, 42, 43
business, 54

camera, 11
certification, 56
client, 4, 6
closing out the case, 48
clothing, 32
conflict of interest, 31
contingent outcome, 9
contract, 53
counsel for the opposition, 10, 11, 21
credibility, 30, 31, 60
cross-examintion, 19, 41

decorum, 11
defendant, 5
Defense Research Institute (DRI), 58
demeanor, 31
deposition, 18, 20
direct examination, 39
discovery, 13, 14, 16
discovery methods, 23
doctor bag, 11
dress, 31
DRI Index, 59

engineer, unlicensed, 2
ethical responsibilities, 63
evidence, 12
exhibits, 49
expert status, 60
Expert Witness Index, 58
expertise, 39

Federal Rules of Civil Procedure, 13
fee, 8, 9, 51, 52
fee charged to opposing counsel, 54
Fifth Amendment rights to silence, 25, 26
fishing expedition, 24
fixed fee, 52
forensic practice, 60
Forensic Services Directory, 58, 59

gestures, 32

hypothetical questions, 35

impartiality, 41
impeachment, 23, 29, 45
inconsistency, 48
incriminating questions, 25
insurance company, 5, 53
interrogatory, 16
investigation, 9

job of the expert witness, 6
jurors, 40

lay witnesses, 38
leading the witness, 39
legal procedure, 55
license, 2
lump sum payment, 52

management, 61
manner, 36
models, 12

National Academy of Forensic
    Engineers (NAFE), 57
National Bureau of Standards, 12
National Forensic Center, 58, 59
National Society of Professional
    Engineers (NSPE), 57
notes, 41

objection, 46
opinion, 21, 41
opposing counsel, 19, 43

per diem fee, 9, 52
photographic record, 11
photographs, 11, 41
physical evidence, 10
plaintiff, 5
pre-deposition conference, 19, 20
preliminary investigation, 7, 8
pretrial discovery procedure, 6
pretrial jitters, 36
privileged communication, 15
privileged material, 17
product liability, 3
professional license, 2

professional societies, 55
protective order, 27

qualifications, 30, 37, 41, 42
quality assurance program, 12

rapid-fire questions, 44
records, 11
recross examination, 47, 48
redirect examination, 47, 48
referral, 57
Register of Expert Witnesses, 58
report, 13
reputation, 55
resume, 37, 55
retainer fee, 52
right to a protective order, 27
right to a subpoena, 26
rights as a witness, 24
Rule #26, 23, 24, 27
Rule #30, 28
Rule #30(e), 29
rules of Civil Procedure, 23
rules of evidence, 38

screening the case, 51
self-contradiction, 19
shouting, 47

slang expressions, 33
societies, 55
subpoena, 16
subpoena duces tecum, 17
surprise witness, 14

taking the Fifth, 25
tape recorder, 11
testifying in court, 34
testimony, 42
testimony, after, 46
tone of voice, 32
trade secrets, 27
transcript of a deposition, 22
trick questions, 45

United States Supreme Court, 23
unlicensed engineer, 2

waiving reading, 23
waiving signature, 28, 29
Westlaw's Computer-based Forensic
    Services Directory, 58, 59
Who's Who in Engineering, 58
work product, 15
work product doctrine, 15